GUERRILLA WEALTH

The Tactical Secrets of the Wealthy ... Finally Revealed

By

Jay Conrad Levinson
and
Loral Langemeier

GUERRILLA WEALTH

"Guerrilla Wealth is a refreshing new approach to wealth building in today's economy. The simple, clear wealth strategies are backed up by tactics that anyone can put into practice immediately. Jay and Loral take the mystery out of becoming financially free and provide worksheets in each chapter to methodically move the reader through the process. It's like a seminar between two covers."

Brian Tracy
Brian Tracy International

"For years I have been teaching people that working is the very worst way to earn money ... now I can tell them that Guerilla Wealth explains the very best way. It's tremendous that Loral and Jay have come together to co-author this book. They are two brilliant individuals and their combined knowledge will help any serious student to earn millions of dollars. This is the kind of book you should give to your friends."

Bob Proctor
Chairman, LifeSuccess Productions

"Loral offers a clear and innovative course of action that could turn even procrastinating wannabes into enthusiastic Guerrilla Wealth Builders."

Rob Black – Wall Street Analyst and
Host of KRON 4's Rob Black and Your Money

"Loral teaches by example. Many people talk about creating wealth, but Loral does it, and helps others fulfill their dreams. She has helped give me the confidence to succeed way beyond the basketball court. I am investing in my future, growing, and building everyday."

Jennifer Azzi, Olympic Gold Medalist

"Guerrilla Wealth will change your life! The tools and insights in this book are invaluable and incredibly practical. If you want more money in your life, read this book immediately. Loral's straightforward guidance will get you on the path to living the life you've always dreamed."

Jill Lublin
Best Selling Author: Guerrilla
Publicity and Networking Magic

"Loral, I congratulate you on Guerrilla Wealth. You and Jay have created the ideal handbook for individuals trying to shake loose of outdated thinking to cash-in on the tidal wave of opportunity in the Information Age. You've really nailed it!"

John V Childers, National Speaker/Trainer

"This book will change your mind, reprogram your brain and help you to discover how to build your bank account FAST. If you are shamelessly serious about building wealth and financial freedom, grab a copy, sit down and read it word for word!"

Debbie Allen
Author of Confessions of Shameless Self Promoters

ISBN #: 0-9727253-9-3

Live Out Loud, Inc.
P.O. Box 10151
San Rafael, CA
94912
www.liveoutloud.com
www.loralsbigtable.com

To place additional orders, please call
888-262-2402
Email: orders@liveoutloud.com

TABLE OF CONTENTS

DEDICATION

To my son,
Logan Christian Langemeier,
for all he has done to show me
a vivid imagination,
a healthy perspective
and a love that is
unconditional for life.

Thank you.

I love you.

ACKNOWLEDGEMENTS

Thank you to everyone who has touched my life and made this book possible.

First, to my son, Logan, who is my inspiration.

To my family who has cheered me on and been a backbone for my growth, for my persistence and for my courage. Specifically, my Mom and Dad, Jeff, Doug, Kent and Holly. My Aunt Bev, who always told me to "Go for it!."

To my extended "California" family - Dianne, Shea, Gabby, Clare, Tim, Robert, Jim and Serene. Without them I never would have had the opportunity and quiet to write this book.

To my wonderful co-author Jay Conrad Levinson for believing in my work and allowing me the prestige and honor of joining his Guerrilla Team.

To Jill Lublin for insisting that Jay and I would make a great collaborative team and facilitating our meeting.

To Mark Steisel, Gina Hayden, Randy Peyser, Rick Miller and Patti Knoles for taking my thoughts, words, concepts and actions and helping me to frame them in a way that offers value, insight and education to the largest audience.

To Anita and Lew Williams for making sure that what is "Loral" and what is "Live Out Loud" was not lost in the editorial process.

To my incredible mentors - Bob Proctor, Jay Conrad Levinson, Sandy Botkin, Mark Victor Hansen and Brian Tracy - who have taught me innumerable lessons and invaluable skills.

To the Live Out Loud Team - Shannon, Kris, Gayle, Heather, Aaryn, Sandi, Mandy, Rob, Stephanie and Andrea - for keeping the wheels of this operation turning. To those who have been on the team: Chris, Jen, Mike, Kati and Mark, my attorney, who keeps me on track.

To the Live Out Loud Coaches - Will, Virginia, Robin, Veronica, Barbara, Melanie, Dawn, Sheila, Socorro, Shawn, Jay and Paul - for taking my work to the public and proving, one client at a time, that it works and that success is achievable.

And of course to each and every Live Out Loud client, especially those in Loral's Big Table, for trusting me with their lives and their success and allowing me to perfect my work on living, breathing, dynamic individuals.

And, to the numerous people who have impacted my life and growth. A few of them are Ernestine, Deb and Dan, Alex, Jon, Keith, Vicki and Joseph, John, Jeff, Sue, Kat, Melinda, Christian and Kelly, plus others who are too numerous to be named.

God bless you all.

Thank you.

BIOGRAPHIES

Jay Conrad Levinson, creator of the Guerrilla series of best-selling marketing books, has teamed with Loral Langemeier to bring highly effective, unconventional guerrilla tactics to wealth building. President of his own marketing and consulting firm, he lectures nationwide on Guerrilla business techniques for major corporations, professional organizations and universities. He lives in San Rafael, California.

Loral Langemeier, founder of Live Out Loud is known as the "millionaire maker". A team made multi-millionaire by age 35 she actively invests in business, the market, multiple real estate ventures and more. Through her diverse experience, she developed the concept of a Financial Wealth Cycle which is the core of her coaching programs. President of several companies, Loral is a nationally known speaker, coach and author. She lives with her son Logan in Nevada.

READY?

STOP!

The information provided in this book does not constitute legal or accounting advice or opinions, and should not be relied upon as such. It is provided solely and exclusively for general, non-specific educational purposes, and to advise readers of the general nature of the ways to build wealth.

Your financial planning must be specifically tailored to your own particular needs and circumstances, and it could be dangerous to apply the general information in this book without seeking professional guidance. *The information in this book is not a substitute for professional legal or financial advice, so consult with an experienced professional who is licensed in your state before attempting any planning techniques described or alluded to in this book.*

You should also be aware that any attempt to defeat the collection of certain U.S. government and U.S. government-backed obligations could subject you to criminal sanctions.

FOREWORD

My co-author of this book and I have something very important in common. We've both learned that successful people have specialized knowledge and a fervent desire, and that they take decisive action.

We've also learned that many well-meaning people who have success and wealth on their minds have the knowledge they need, have that vision that propels them forward, but never quite get around to taking the necessary action. Building a Wealth Cycle might seem to be a daunting, intimidating and scary job. However, Loral and I have created a series of tasks that are much simpler, much smaller and best of all, far more conducive for you to take action. That way, wealth will come easier. That's one of the winning characteristics of guerrilla wealth.

The techniques and tactics you'll need to actually attain your goal are in two very crucial places; one of them is in this book. The other is within yourself. This book can show you exactly how to tap those wellsprings of strength and confidence.

Some books will take you part of the way toward wealth. This book will take you all the way. It will take you there with certainty, with simplicity and with the experience of others who have done just what you want to do.

To be sure, Loral Langemeier and I will lead the way for you, and take you by the hand from a mindset that embraces scarcity to a mindset that embraces abundance. This book will give you a step-by-step roadmap from your limitations to the achievement of your most ambitious dreams and goals.

Unlike many books which tell you what you need to know, this book really and truly forces you to take the actions that lead to wealth. Sound tough? Well, it is tough, at least at first, but it's also fun . . . great fun . . . because we have made it fun. The secrets that lead to great wealth do not have to be boring.

This book will ask a lot of you, but it gives you far more than it asks.

You are not about to read a book about theory. You are not about to read a book about statistics. And you certainly are not about to read a book of case histories – tales of others who have done what you want to do – without also getting the how-to information they used.

Instead – and I direct this thought to your cellular level – this is a book about you, a book about where you want to go and how to get there. There are only two parts to becoming wealthy and maintaining that cycle of wealth. The first part is this book. The second part is the actions you will take to give wings to your dreams. Loral and I are not only your wealth mentors in these pages. We are also your partners. We look forward to leading you down the path to guerrilla wealth . . . and walking beside you every step of the way. It's going to be a rewarding journey.

Jay Conrad Levinson
Marin County, California
Author, *Guerrilla Marketing* series of books
Over 14 million sold; now in 41 languages

INTRODUCTION

Successful, wealthy people are those who build their assets . . .
and then they build their lifestyles.

Do you want to become truly wealthy in every sense of the word? Do you want to create and live the life of your dreams? Whether this means making $30,000 per year at your job or making millions upon millions in real estate, you've come to the right place.

However, if you're counting on winning the lottery or solving your money problems with a trip to Las Vegas, this isn't the right place for you. Lottery thinking is a totally different mindset from what you'll learn in this book. This may seem obvious, but we're amazed at the number of people we talk to – smart, educated people – who make statements that betray their own version of lottery thinking. "We'll just hang in there and everything will turn out somehow." Or "As soon as 'X' happens, we'll be on top of things." Unless you're pro-actively, consciously building wealth according to a *plan*, don't count on anything turning out on its own. Success is never an accident.

We're also not going to tell you how to outsmart the stock market and hit the long-shot IPO that will make you a millionaire overnight. That's an appealing thought, and one that almost seems rational when someone you know picks the right one. Even we know someone whose father became a millionaire because he bought Dell Computer Corporation's stock when it first came out and then watched it shoot through the roof. But these "success" stories can't be duplicated with any certainty because they aren't the result of a *systematic approach for building wealth.*

In *Guerrilla Wealth*, we aren't interested in luck, lotteries or get-rich-quick schemes. We're interested in giving you the tools to get out of debt if necessary, and then the skills to acquire wealth, protect it and accelerate its growth in a predictable, yet aggressive way.

You don't have to be "lucky" to get a tidy lump sum of money in your lifetime. For Boomers, the money will probably come in the form of inheritance from their parents' estates. You thought only the trust-fund babies of the rich and super-rich were going to have chunks of cash and assets fall into their laps? Think again! Boomers are poised to inherit $10 trillion in cash and assets. When you know the guerrilla tactics we'll teach you in this book, you'll be ready to make something of that money and not watch it slip through your fingers.

Perhaps you're one of the many people building your wealth through their own businesses or investments. If that's the case, we can help you be even more focused, more on point to achieve your financial goal faster.

The truth is that the majority of people don't fit into either of these groups. The majority of people don't become wealthy. They work day in and day out struggling to pay bills, stay out of debt and just get ahead for at least one pay period.

If that's you, it's time to change your game plan. You see, it doesn't matter which of the situations we've described applies to you. The potential to build wealth is available to everyone in this country. Once you absorb the specialized knowledge and master some vital skills, you can thrive, even in today's economy.

The prime example of this is Donald Trump. Not so long ago, he was over $750 million dollars in debt! Now look at him. Despite his occasional troubles, he's on top of the world. Trump has constantly proven that he's not afraid to take risks. #He has rebuilt his financial empire and has mentored others to obtain great wealth. He did it with knowledge and by following a system that works. And if it all fell apart tomorrow, Trump, with his knowledge, could rebuild it all again.

This skill set is exactly what we're going to go over, step by step by step, in this book. The skill set to start from EXACTLY WHERE YOU ARE and get you to EXACTLY WHERE YOU WANT TO BE. We call this skill set Wealth Building.

Now let us tell you what this skill set is not. It's not a template. It's not a "follow steps A-B-C to get to D" system.

Why do we bring this up? It's important because most people's current relationship to success, whether it be about money or not, started when they were young. Our educational system has conditioned us to memorize and regurgitate information. If we memorized the information we were given and repeated it back on a test, we were rewarded with an A. This was success. Then we went on to get a job where we produced a project to get approval to get a raise. Again, success. This was success based on what we call a template: A + B = C.

The need for approval, the need for permission and the need for a template in today's society still prevail. Everyone now seems to want the same sure-fire, easily understood, step-by-step, foolproof formula that they can follow to get what they want.

Today, people want templates for finding the perfect mate, bringing up their children, buying, furnishing and maintaining their homes, and finding fame and fortune. They're looking for a simple recipe that will tell them how to bake an elaborate, professional-looking wedding cake with the cheapest of ingredients and no baking experience.

Unfortunately, the same ideas have been applied to wealth. We've found, after working with thousands of people, that the vast majority still want a template, or a magic pill, they can easily swallow. If, like good little students, they follow the template to the letter, they think they'll be rewarded with financial security and get an "A" in life.

This book takes a different approach: it's about creating personalized, strategic plans. It is not about creating or following templates. *Templates* work for EVERYONE to some degree; however, a *plan* works for YOU specifically!

Wealth cannot be acquired haphazardly or by accident. Perhaps more than any other thing you'll ever do, building wealth requires a plan. A plan is different than a template. A plan is a customized, unique application of a step-by-step process. This process is what we're going to give you in *Guerrilla Wealth*.

Why are we laying out this plan for you? We're laying it out because when it comes to making money, many of the respected blueprints are long out of date. They fail to offer solutions to today's challenges because they're based on yesterday's thinking. We call that thinking the traditional, old, "Industrial Age model," and it no longer makes sense.

Guerrilla Wealth is about changing your relationship to the traditional, Industrial Age model of creating financial success. The guerrilla approach is about developing an attitude. It's reconditioning yourself to see the possibilities, instead of the problems. It's about being assertive, self-directed and passionate in your desire to acquire wealth. It requires being extremely resourceful, knowing how to use all the necessary tools, and working with the top people to bring you a lifetime of sustainable wealth.

A new concept that we would like to introduce you to in this book is *Guerrilla Accountability,* which is your personal responsibility to:

 ➤ Plan what you will do.

 ➤ Do it.

 ➤ By when?

 ➤ At what standard?

> ➢ You must also identify and declare who will hold you accountable for what it is you say you want and what you will do to achieve it.

In *Guerrilla Wealth*, we'll introduce you to a well-tested system for building a lifetime of wealth that really works. As a Guerrilla Wealth Builder, you'll need to know and implement these seven tactical steps that the wealthy were never willing to reveal . . . until now.

1. Your Wealth Conditioning

2. Your Financial Baseline

3. Your Financial Freedom Day

4. Managing Your LifeStyle Cycle™

5. Building a Wealth Cycle™ Foundation

6. Acceleration of Your Wealth Cycles

7. Leadership of Your Wealth Team

Much like a recipe, these steps need to be followed in order. You need a solid foundation before you create the acceleration of your wealth. If not, you're putting your money on an unstable foundation. We want you to grow your wealth from a comprehensive base.

If you aren't where you want to be, it's likely you did something that is very common. You used your income to create a lifestyle – the homes, cars, clothes, boats, vacations or other symbols of affluence – that stands or falls on your earned income alone. Wealthy people build their assets first, then create a lifestyle that isn't the mere appearance of affluence, but based on real wealth.

Now that you know what to expect from this book, we request that you read it slowly and carefully. Then, do the exercises, just as you would if you were in a coaching session. Don't proceed until you understand what you've just read. Let the concepts sink in, because they're the building blocks of your wealth knowledge. Examine how you could apply each concept to your own personal situation and how it could work for you. Get the basics down in order to build your financial foundation. Go at your own pace, take your time and remember that you're not in a race.

This book is just the beginning; it's your wealth-building starting point. It will teach you the basics and start you on the road to wealth. Feel free to contact us at Live Out Loud (www.LiveOutLoud.com), where we offer a wide variety of personal financial coaching programs, courses and expert strategies that can build your wealth.

Jay Conrad Levinson
Loral Langemeier

September 2004

Section I

YOUR
CONDITIONING

I

The Wealth Conversation

"Money is the last conversational taboo."

Ready. Go! The first thing we're going to teach you is how to Live Out Loud by getting you into the conversation about money. To Live Out Loud is the very essence of being a guerrilla, if only because it's so foreign to most people.

At one level, it means speaking openly, honestly, directly and decisively in a solution-oriented manner about all aspects of your life. It's about not hiding skeletons in the closet, sweeping uncomfortable issues under the rug, or ignoring the things you're not able to face.

It means you're going to learn how to talk about your dreams, your plans, your vision . . . about money and wealth-building.

In a society where "nice" people traditionally have not talked about money in polite company, this is a new concept. Some unspoken law decreed that the topic of money was taboo, especially for women! So we seldom, if ever, discussed subjects that would become central in our lives: money and finances. But talking is vitally important to your success. Why? First, it calls you out of hiding.

No more half-made plans that you never share and that you never quite commit yourself to. When you Live Out Loud, you're accountable to yourself and others. Finally, you'll dig around in your attic of lost

3

dreams and pull out the ones that - if realized - will utterly transform your life. When you Live Out Loud, you get to sort and recognize the dreams that have been harbored in your heart, perhaps as early as childhood.

You need - and we mean need - to hear your own words from your own mouth announce to yourself what your dreams are. Something happens when you do. That something starts making the dream real inside you, and outside as well. When others hear your dream loud and clear, they can cheer you on, offer substantial help (referrals, resources, etc.) and keep that dream in front of you.

You need to understand money is only a tool. Making and accumulating money is useless unless you have a purpose for it. What's yours? An education for your kids? Contributions to your church or favorite cause? Sure, you may dream of a lake house or splashy new car, but intuitively we know that's just stuff. Nice stuff, but just stuff. Our real satisfaction comes from doing something significant with our money.

If you currently aren't financially stable - or are even deeply in debt - the idea of accomplishing much more than paying the bills may be off your radar. But you must understand that, without a compelling dream, making money will lose its appeal. You won't have the excitement to learn more, do more or be with people who are on the same track. Without a dream, it simply isn't worth it.

Go ahead. Allow your mind to start letting those dreams, almost-forgotten plans and even outrageous

The Wealth Conversation

"what ifs" start bubbling to the top of your brain. The journey we've begun together can transform your life. There's no greater transformation than becoming the person you hoped you could be. Money is not its own end. It's just a means to an end. And while money is not the most important thing in life, money does have more impact on every area of your life than anything else.

If talking about money is hard, talking about dreams and aspirations can be even harder. That's why we'll teach you how to have a new conversation about money.

This is key to your success.

Compare that kind of approach with how our society deals with health and fitness. America is obsessed with health and fitness. It's in the news, in magazines, on TV, in the stores. We dress in fitness gear to go almost everywhere. Consumers speak with authority on recent medical studies, using the correct scientific terminology. We talk about diets with our friends. We're familiar with complex medical procedures. People have no problem revealing the most intimate details of their health to perfect strangers.

As health and fitness govern our physical lives, money and finances affect our economic lives. Ironically, in today's material world, more people measure themselves by the yardstick of their wealth than by their health. Yet, money and finances are seldom discussed except in the most impersonal terms. We'll talk about some news item about consumer debt or investments, but we'll rarely hear someone talking about their own indebtedness or portfolio.

So that's the first thing we'll change.

If saying it out loud is the first step, saying it out loud in a life-changing/action-oriented way is another. That's why we're going to give you a whole new vocabulary to talk about money. This new language will let you form a positive and healthy relationship with money, instead of a negative, uncomfortable relationship that you avoid. Don't be fooled, though. We haven't just changed the words. As we go through the book together, you'll learn that the very meaning behind the words and the actions that are required of them is radically different.

Why do we need a new vocabulary and a new way of dealing with money? Even though we are well into the new millennium - surrounded by amazing technologies, remarkable breakthroughs and new understandings - we are still following tired, old, financial theories and success models. Believe it or not, the Industrial Age model for financial success is still the driving force in today's finance and business arenas. So what is the Industrial Age model?

THE INDUSTRIAL AGE MODEL

Jane Bryant Quinn is a fabulous writer and financial expert. In *Making The Most Of Your Money* (Simon & Schuster, 1997), she outlined how people normally lived under the traditional Industrial Age model. This

The Wealth Conversation

way of life has been so ingrained, so unquestioned, it's easy to understand how we've dragged it forward.

We're about to challenge the norm, so see how closely your life has tracked with this old model.

Ages 20 to 30

> ➤ establish credit to buy furniture, appliances, or a car
> ➤ learn about insurance
> ➤ discover how taxes affect your net income
> ➤ save for a down payment or borrow from parents to buy a house
> ➤ start a retirement account at your job

Ages 31 to 45

> ➤ seemingly endless spending on family expenses
> ➤ continue retirement fund contributions through automatic paycheck withdrawals
> ➤ borrow against home equity to finance life
> ➤ start a business or get more education in hopes of financial stability

Ages 46 to 55

> ➤ college tuition for children
> ➤ jolted into seriously preparing for retirement

Ages 56 to 65

> ➤ empty nest, more disposable income
> ➤ prepare for retirement with increased savings

The Wealth Conversation

Ages 66 to 75
> ➤ live on pension from job, Social Security
> ➤ let savings grow until later

Ages 76 and Up
> ➤ spend, even from capital, and assume the kids will plan for themselves

Let us bottom-line this for you. 90 percent of the people on this planet grow up doing exactly what their parents did. If you believed you had to work hard for money, because that's what your parents had to do, it became your orientation towards money. If you were encouraged to go to school, get good grades, and get a good job with a good company for the rest of your life, that's what you did.

In most cases, you probably took the same approaches as your parents and became pretty much what they wanted you to become. Their limits were your limits. Their lack of financial savvy became yours. This isn't a judgment of our parents. In the absence of proper education (and people actually talking Out Loud about money issues), they did the best they could. And the game just continues on pretty much the same.

During the ages of 20 to 30 - early in your career - you start learning how to make money and establish credit. You probably buy some cool stuff and reinforce the conditioning with which you were raised. Between your 20s and 30s, you either break out of the mold and start generating more wealth or you stay in the mold by getting a good job and saving in qualified plans for your retirement. Then again, you may start looking at the entrepreneurial way of life.

When you hit your 30s or 40s, you probably have kids, get a bigger house and buy more cars. You also probably start to accumulate lots of consumer debt, and you still have college tuition looming ahead. As you grow older, you need to look at long-term care insurance and your parents could be coming to live with you. Between 30 and 45, we get bombarded and then we enter the top earning years of life. If you're still working for a company, your wealth is probably not accumulating quickly. If you're an entrepreneur, you've probably stepped on the gas by now.

Jane's model is accurate. It stems from the adage, "go to school, get good grades, get a good job and you'll be secure." The Industrial Age taught us that the ethic of hard work, machinery, grit and grind was the norm. Even today, in the Information Age, we're still conditioned to believe that the government or our company will take care of us in our golden years. We're not allowed to access qualified money (retirement savings) until we're close to sixty. Traditionally, financial planning tools are designed for us to begin acquiring wealth when we're in our fifties, sixties and seventies.

The problem is that you basically can't touch your retirement funds until you turn 59-and-a-half. So while you age, watch your family grow, and see the world change, your money just sits - during rain or shine, economic ups and downs, and changes in your life. Your money is locked in. It's unavailable to you. You can't even get the interest, so you can't take advantage of opportunities that may arise. If you do use the limited options to access the money, you face severe penalties.

And as you and your money sit and wait, what are those nice people doing who are holding your money? They're investing; they're using YOUR money to make themselves money. They're doing what you could be doing, but for a lesser percentage of return. Sure, they throw you some crumbs in the form of interest while they make the big dough and collect their management fees and commissions.

Now, we don't know about you, but we're not sold on the idea of working a lifetime and saving lots of money, but not being able to access it or enjoy it until we're at retirement's doorstep. To us, that's like buying a cool new car and having to wait until your hair turns white in order to drive it. We want to drive in prime time; to use OUR money when WE want it or need it. If you're working hard and making money, do you really want to wait 15, 20, 30 or even 35 years to get it?

We certainly don't!

We want you to have all YOUR hard-earned cash at YOUR disposal now, or when YOU want it. We want you to own businesses now and to exercise greater flexibility over how you invest your money. We also don't want you to hand over so much of your earnings to the government.

If you feel the same, you must make some changes. You must learn how to invest differently and to use your business to help you grow. It's time to discard your outmoded Industrial Age models and change the way you think and approach financial success. As we explained in the beginning of this chapter, the first thing you must do is change your conversations about money.

The model for the current Information Age promotes young entrepreneurialism, young wealth, young investors and risk taking. Even if you aren't considered young, you can use the Information Age model to secure your future and build wealth. Yes, you can.

THE CONVERSATION

To get you out of that old, Industrial Age thinking that's been holding you back, we want to engage you in a new conversation about financial success.

So let's talk!

Since we're not taught to Live Out Loud about money, it stands to reason that we're not equipped with the proper mindset or tools to learn, acquire, manage or grow our finances. Why should we be? Did any of those who conditioned you teach you:

- ➤ The basics of personal finance?
- ➤ The proper use of credit and credit cards?
- ➤ The basic use of cash management?
- ➤ How to write and balance a forecast?
- ➤ How to balance your checkbook online?
- ➤ How to create a profit & loss statement?

The Wealth Conversation

➤ How to read a balance sheet?
➤ How to pay your bills systematically?
➤ How to incorporate for the highest tax strategies?
➤ How to invest your money so it compounds?
➤ How to build and lead your wealth team?

If you answered "Yes" to even one of these questions, you're in a tiny minority. Only three to five percent of the population has created "real wealth." To join this minority, begin to hold conversations about money daily and out loud.

Since so many theories about wealth and money are ingrained in the old, Industrial Age model, we need to start our conversation by teaching you a new vocabulary. Once you learn these new terms and develop a wealth-building vocabulary, you can shed those old, Industrial Age ideas and start your excursion into these modern, Information Age, wealth-building times. This is where we seriously start moving away from the way most people teach wealth concepts and start moving into the guerrilla tactics.

The Wealth Conversation

INDUSTRIAL AGE Vocabulary	VS.	INFORMATION AGE Vocabulary
Balancing Your Checkbook	VS.	Financial Baseline
Budgeting	VS.	Forecasting
Consumer Debt	VS.	LifeStyle Cycle
Retirement	VS.	Freedom Day
Sole Proprietor and W-2 Wage Earners	VS.	Wealth Cycle Foundation
Financial Planning	VS.	Acceleration of Wealth Cycles
Financial Advisors	VS.	Your Wealth Team
Get Rich Quick	VS.	Sustainable Wealth Cycles
Template	VS.	Plan

Balancing Your Checkbook—It's a common misconception that if you've balanced your checkbook, you'll know exactly where you stand financially. In truth, that's a fallacy. Although balancing your checkbook is essential, it only tells you a small part of what we call your Financial Baseline. It just tells you how much money you have in the bank, not how profitable you are. Your financial baseline includes your income and expenses and your assets and liabilities. It lets you know exactly where you are financially, and more specifically, how much money it takes for you to live the type of life you want on a daily basis.

Budgeting—We don't like this word. Doesn't it make you think of dieting? The word "budgeting" has a negative connotation, and both budgeting and dieting are limiting. No one does it, so let's change the conversation. Budgeting is the placing of limitations that tell you what you cannot do. We challenge you to instead Forecast what you can do - to deliberately and purposefully plan out step by step how you will spend your money. On the surface, the distinction may seem insignificant or simply a matter of semantics. However, we assure you that the differences are major and that thinking in terms of forecasting, rather than budgeting, is a massively powerful tool.

Consumer Debt—Talk about a negative connotation ... we've all been taught to avoid consumer debt! So instead of consumer debt, we call it a LifeStyle Cycle. Your chosen lifestyle - those daily choices that you make concerning how you spend your money - affects your ability to create financial success. The house you own, the clothes you wear, the school your children attend, the car you drive, the take-out food you eat and the Starbucks that you constantly drink impact your wealth. Maybe none of these individual items will put you into debt, but they do cost money that could be used more effectively elsewhere.

The Wealth Conversation

Retirement—As we alluded to before, the commonly accepted wisdom is that you work until a certain age and retire - not necessarily because you want to or can afford to, but because you have reached retirement age. We challenge you to forgo retirement, and instead, create a Financial Freedom Day. A Financial Freedom Day is the day when you will stop working, not because you have to, but because you have deliberately planned and taken the appropriate financial actions that will let you live the life you want.

Sole Proprietor & W-2 Wage Earners—The Industrial Age model encouraged people to fit into one of two categories: either the W-2 wage earner or a sole proprietor. The challenge with this model is that it's very difficult to become wealthy because you're paying too much money in taxes. Everyone that we know who has become truly wealthy has done it inside a corporate structure, taking full advantage of the highest tax-savings benefits allowed by law. We're not saying that it's wrong to have a job; we are saying that you can do this AND learn to take full advantage of incorporation and tax strategies to hold on to more of your hard-earned money. We're going to show you how to use the new concept - Wealth Cycle Foundation - even as you keep your day job.

Financial Planning—Traditional financial planning tries to make sure that you'll make 80 percent of your earning capacity at retirement. Compare this to having the ability to create wealth at any age and progressively create more as you get older. We don't know about you, but who wants to limit their income and be poorer when we get older? Traditional financial planning typically looks at investment options such as stocks, bonds, mutual funds and insurance options, whereas our Acceleration of Wealth Cycles encourages a broader diversification of non-traditional investments, such as real estate, gas and oil, private placements, private notes and more. The model we use isn't geared just toward long-term investments. We're interested in cash, cash flow, and equity outcomes.

Financial Advisors—In the Industrial Age model, traditional financial advisors are treated as expert money managers who will take care of your money for you. This is what we call the "park and pray method." You park your money with them and pray that they make you more. Typically, they have a template that they use for the majority of their clients, and they occupy the driver's seat. In our model, you're in the driver's seat. We want you to lead Your Wealth Team, which means that you clearly identify your individual specialized plan and pro-actively interview, hire and direct the team that creates your strategy for creating wealth. Your team should be comprised of individuals whom you selected for their expertise in specific areas, and they should clearly support your goals, not their pocket books.

Get Rich Quick—Quite frankly there is no such thing; it does not happen! History is filled with many fool-proof, guaranteed, get-rich schemes that promised fast and easy wealth. Many of them sounded so good, so tempting, but usually only the promoters made money, not the investors. When you invest in schemes that are

The Wealth Conversation

fast and easy, your money can disappear just as fast and as easily. So we talk about and concentrate on creating Sustainable Wealth Cycles. Sustainable is the key word; it means investments that will continue to provide strong returns that you can depend upon over time.

Templates—We previously discussed templates, and the fact that most people rely upon them. We want to pull you away from template-type thinking and reemphasize that, while a template may work for EVERYONE to some degree, a Plan will work for YOU specifically! Guerrilla Wealth will teach YOU how to construct your master wealth plan.

Now that you have the language you need to hold the conversation, let's begin to LIVE OUT LOUD!

SUCCESS STORIES

Mark Erickson

"I met Loral when I was on unemployment and had nearly $80,000 in credit card debt. My wife had a regular W-2 job and we believed that money was not a renewable resource. We were people who believed in holding steady jobs, working for others, and I was afraid of taking big risks. Although I was interested in real estate investing, I needed to learn the nuts and bolts of how it worked.

Loral introduced me to investment strategies, the

The Wealth Conversation

pros and cons of entity structuring and the advantages of separating my personal debt and business income. I learned that no one else would do it for me; that if I started playing to win, instead of not playing to lose, I had to be willing to take calculated risks. I also learned that if I failed, I could do it again.

Through Loral, I met others who taught me that money is a renewable resource if you plan and take steps to make it happen. This convinced my wife and me to make lifestyle shifts and change our thinking about how we ran our lives. We started to operate more like a business, to make business connections and build a strong wealth team. We now associate with people who share our ideas about building wealth. When I didn't have the confidence to flip the first house I bought, people who had flipped houses helped me and I ended up making money. In the last 18 months, I've invested in foreclosures and have generated over $250,000 in income. I've paid all my debt in full. Now, when I sell a house, I make as much as $90,000.

This last year has been a true leap of faith. My confidence has increased and I think about the creation of wealth completely differently. I now have no doubt that if I stick it out and follow what I've learned from Loral, I'll succeed."

SUMMING UP

In our material world, people tend to measure themselves by their wealth, but somehow money and finances are seldom discussed. The subject is taboo. We want to change that and get you into a wealth conversation. We want you to Live Out Loud about your dreams, your hopes, the bills, investment opportunities, college funds and gas money.

Creating wealth starts with a conversation. Unfortunately, the few conversations you have probably had about money used terms with negative implications. These old, Industrial Age terms impose limits that restrict how you think and act in regard to money and the creation of wealth.

If you seriously want to build wealth, discard the old, Industrial Age terms and their built-in limits. Come into the Information Age and replace that old language with a positive Information Age vocabulary that will expand your vision and your outlook about creating wealth. In the process, you'll be removing many of the roadblocks that have been preventing you from becoming wealthy.

LORAL'S LEARNING LOOP

A word from Loral:

As we end this first chapter, I want to introduce you to a unique concept that I challenge you to find in any other book. It's used in ALL of my live training sessions and coaching programs. It's called the Learning and Accountability Loop . . . Guerrilla Accountability.

I firmly believe that the first step you made on the path to success was to pick up this book and begin to read it. That alone will begin to produce incredible results in your life. However, I know for a FACT that your results will increase infinitely if you begin to formulate and draw out a plan of how to put each of the steps and concepts that we are teaching you into ACTION. I require this of all my students and now I'm asking you to do the exercises completely to get the most from this entire journey toward wealth.

So, here is your first Learning Loop. Go ahead and write directly in this book. Don't worry about it.

What are three things you learned from this chapter?

_____

_____

_____

_____

_____

_____

_____

_____

_____

_____

What three actions will you take as a result of this chapter?

_____

_____

_____

_____

_____

_____

List the dates when you will begin and complete your three actions.

_____

_____

_____

To whom will you be accountable?

_____

_____

2

Your Financial Conditioning: Your Personal Money Psychology

"First we unlearn. Then we can learn."

Things are about to get very interesting! Before we can teach you and lead you to your own wealth, we need to help you unlearn all the wrong notions, incorrect assumptions and false ideas about money. We call these the myths, mysteries and misconceptions about money. They have to go. If we don't get rid of them, it'll be like having termites in the basement. They'll just chew away in the dark until your structure is weakened. And you may never realize what happened.

You see, it's really important to understand that your beliefs about money - even the wrong-headed ones - show up in your life. So if you've tried to improve your finances before without rooting out the negative comments you heard at home, or the fiercely held beliefs of poor old Uncle Harry, or your teachers, preachers and other authority figures, you're stuck.

This isn't news to you. It's fairly common for anyone teaching financial principles to address the issue of past conditioning. We're all aware that our formative years - up to about age eight - are key to forming our personal "truth" about money.

What's different about *Guerrilla Wealth* is that we're addressing more than your personal conditioning based on your individual experience. We have to break the limitations of the entire Industrial Age model of wealth. Otherwise your wealth-building efforts would be like driving a 1930s car on today's interstate highways. That means taking on some deeply held cultural norms as well as your own personal baggage. Some of what you were taught or just absorbed under that system wasn't even true then. It certainly isn't true now. Trying to move ahead without disassembling these beliefs practically guarantees you won't enjoy the freedom you're after.

Some of these outdated beliefs may include:

➢ Money is the root of all evil.
➢ A penny saved is a penny earned.
➢ Money is dirty.
➢ You must sell your soul for money.
➢ Women are not worthy of money.
➢ Never dip into your savings.
➢ We can't afford it.
➢ We don't deserve money.
➢ Mommy and Daddy will pay for everything.
➢ I am entitled.
➢ My trust fund will pay for it.

All of these beliefs are part of a "scarcity mindset." This mindset creates a vicious cycle that forms what we call "paradigms."

PARADIGMS

We all take the things that we've been conditioned to believe, such as our scarcity mindsets, and build upon them. We construct paradigms, which are examples or patterns that we follow. They govern the way we spend, save and invest, and how we think about and deal with money. Loral's longtime mentor, Bob Proctor, is a master at explaining how our paradigms influence our behavior. Pay close attention to what he has to say.

"Paradigms, what are they? Is the term a buzzword for the Information Age? Absolutely not! Paradigms could be controlling virtually every move you make. When you understand how to build a paradigm that will lawfully guarantee the progressive realization of your worthy ideal, a paradigm to replace the one that presently controls your life, you will have opened a door to a brand new world where you may freely begin to express your power."

In other words, the paradigms we create dictate how we handle our finances. Therefore, we must build new paradigms that will get us what we want. We like to think of them as programs that were downloaded into our brains, programs that were probably written by good people who sincerely wanted nothing but the best for us or the culture and society prevalent in the last century. As a result, many of us are still running our financial lives according to these old models.

Reflect upon the first years of your life. Think of the environment in which you were raised and the people who surrounded you. Think about how they viewed the wealthy, like the industrial leaders.

How did they approach money, finances and wealth?

➢ Did they view them negatively, conservatively, protectively or fearfully?
➢ Did they look at them in terms of problems, not solutions?
➢ How did they feel about the wealthy, such as those who employed them?
➢ Did they regard them with respect or contempt?
➢ Depending on when you were born, how important was "keeping up with the Joneses?"
➢ Was it generally accepted that your family should be satisfied with its "station" in life?
➢ Were there entrepreneurs in the family? How were they viewed?
➢ How deeply did they embed their messages in you?
➢ Down deep, do you subscribe to their views?

Don't get sidetracked by whether they were good or bad people. No doubt, they had your best interests at heart and did the best they could. Instead, realize that you are an extension of their energy, a byproduct of their habitual way of living, as well as their fears. They're the ones who were responsible for the formation of your paradigms, as well as the culture that dictated commonly held "agreements" about money. But you're the one responsible for changing your paradigms and how you think!

GUERRILLA INTELLIGENCE

The people who wrote your paradigms gave you what they had been given, what they honestly believed to be true. They gave you what worked for them during their lives and under the conditions in which they lived. Unfortunately, most of them had no idea what they were doing, and those who did followed concepts from a different time and a different world. Today, most of those concepts no longer apply. Remember, most of their ideas about money were based on their fears.

Regardless of their intentions, the beliefs they taught you are limiting theories that, if left unchanged, can dictate your financial mindset for the rest of your life.

The Industrial Age model permeated society with a particular understanding of money. The "loyal for life" model bound employees to parental-style corporations. That meant the path to financial security for families was through the employer. Many workers were content in the system and didn't look for much more, since the Industrial Age model fulfilled their hope of the American Dream.

Although these models have been passed to you from generation to generation, you're the only person who can change them. You're the pioneer! This is a new world, a new time!

So now that we have explained to you how your past conditioning is directly affecting your current success, you're probably feeling a little overwhelmed. Don't worry; we have the means by which you can change your past conditioning with the right conditioning program. This conditioning program will begin exercising your money muscles.

EXERCISING YOUR MONEY MUSCLES

We believe that everyone has money muscles . . . they're just atrophied little guys. We need a new wealth conditioning program to re-condition how you think about money. What you focus on and give your attention to, you will create more of.

GUERRILLA TACTIC

Think of money conditioning as the equivalent of a health-conditioning program. For example, what happens when you start an exercise program and begin working your muscles? You get sore; lactic acid builds up and those first few days aren't so great. Over time, however, you build more endurance, gain flexibility and grow stronger. Your muscles tone and your focus really zeros in on reaching your goals. In the process, muscles that you don't work atrophy or waste away from neglect.

GUERRILLA TACTIC (cont'd)

Well, the same thing happens with money. So, in order to start building the money muscles you need, construct a decisive plan, find mentors and take the right action. Atrophy those muscles that no longer serve you and are sabotaging your success. Stop giving attention to what you don't want. If you pay attention to those negative thoughts, they won't go away, but if you ignore them, they'll disappear.

Let's begin to work those muscles!

CHANGE WHAT YOU THINK

If you want to be wealthy, you must break the scarcity mindset. The scarcity mindset is outdated and will prevent you from creating wealth. With that mindset:

> - You play to not lose, when you should be playing to win
> - Your decisions are tentative, instead of being decisive
> - You think in terms of holding onto, preserving and protecting, instead of thinking in terms of growing and expanding
> - You operate on the basis of fear and caution, instead of being excited and enthusiastic

Wealthy people don't think and act because of a

scarcity mindset. They're proactive and create the lives they want to live. Most people play to not lose, which is playing from fear. If you're going to become wealthy, be decisive! Move quickly and aggressively with assurance and determination. Always keep your objectives in sight. Being indecisive is a way of holding back; it's the same as saying "no." When opportunity knocks, move forward and ask, "What's next?"

If you want to break the scarcity mindset, start right now, right here! Change your thinking and adopt a prosperity mindset in order to create the opportunity to Live Out Loud. Raise your financial consciousness, and in turn, influence those around you.

Take Loral's example. Growing up on a huge farm in Nebraska, she was taught that if you want to make money, you have to work hard, which she subsequently found wasn't true. So the message that she had to atrophy to enhance her financial development was "you must work hard for money." At the same time, she had to strengthen the message, "money flows easily, constantly." Loral changed her paradigm when she realized that making money is one of the easiest things to do. Even in a war and a recession economy it's easy to make money! You must believe and focus on your belief and it will come true.

Before we go any further, our question to you is: Will you be the one who breaks the scarcity mindset pattern?

Take some time now to examine your thoughts about money. Let's find out specifically what they are. Write about the conversations you've held with yourself or others. List core messages that you carry with you, including those messages that probably sabotage your efforts to build substantial wealth. The object is for you to become more conscious of how you think about money throughout the day because in order to change, you first must be aware of the concepts that are controlling your behavior.

To identify your financial messages, ask yourself these questions:

> ➤ How did your parents', grandparents' or primary caretakers' ideas about finances make them behave?
> ➤ Did it turn them into big savers or misers?
> ➤ Did they feel that they couldn't afford to buy things?
> ➤ Did they put every cent away for a rainy day?
> ➤ Did they become afraid to invest?
> ➤ Did they impress their fears on you?
> ➤ When you were growing up, did you have conversations about money? If so, how old were you?
> ➤ What was discussed? New shoes for the kids, the cost of braces or saving for college?
> ➤ Who dominated the conversation and most influenced you?
> ➤ Did they give you a positive or negative psychology about money?
> ➤ Do you believe only hard, unpleasant work brings prosperity?
> ➤ What do you discuss in conversations about money today?
> ➤ Did you inherit the scarcity mindset?

Now, write out a list and identify:

1. Which beliefs continue to sabotage you?
    a.   Perhaps you don't trust yourself to make clear decisions.
    b.   You need to be right versus being a learner.
    c.   You prefer to look good, i.e., live in the right neighborhood, have the right car and wear elegant clothing.

2. Based on what you know today, what would you like your thinking about money to be? For example, would you like to be:
    a.   Confident when asking for help?
    b.   Able to feel that you deserve and are worthy of money?
    c.   More willing to learn? If you want to be an earner, you must be a learner.

3. What would you like your conversations about money to be like? Would you want them to be:

    a.   Easy, natural, calming, confident, exciting, daily, purposeful and clear?

Now, do the following exercise. Draw a "T-chart." Place one line across the top of a sheet of a paper and then add a perpendicular line that runs down the center of the page so it looks like the letter "T." On the left side, list the financial messages that you want to atrophy. Then, on the right side, record the financial messages that you want to strengthen. See example on next page.

Your Financial Conditioning: Your Personal Money Psychology

Atrophy	Strengthen
I have to work hard for money.	Money comes to me easily.
I don't trust myself with money.	I know the resources are available.

*"I was always looking outside myself
for strength and confidence
but it comes from within.
It is there all the time."*

Anna Freud

RALT Model

Let's start connecting the dots. In order to do so, we want to share the RALT Model with you. RALT stands for Results, Action, Language and Thinking. This model has helped thousands of our clients expand their financial results. The RALT Model is designed to make you tactically aware and help you develop the type of thinking you need to improve your financial results. Use it each day to build the tools and to align your approach to the rewards you seek. The RALT model will reinforce the fact that you need to change your thinking.

It works like this: your thoughts create your language, your language commits you to take action, and your actions produce your results, which link directly back to how you think. Can you see how this could be a vicious cycle if you don't change your relationship with money?

GUERRILLA INTELLIGENCE

In working in psychology and human behavior, and in the health, leadership and personal development industries, we have learned that limited thinking will reinforce limiting language. Limiting language will influence the actions you take and will create limited results.

Remove the limits. Begin "no limit" thinking. Understand that everything is possible. Expect to confront obstacles, walls that you must scale to reach your objectives. That's where the benefits of building your money muscles kick in; building money muscles and getting rid of restrictive thinking will give you the power, endurance and know-how to clear those hurdles. And, in time, you'll learn to anticipate roadblocks, avoid them and make them disappear.

Your Financial Conditioning: Your Personal Money Psychology

	Limiting Results	Expansive Results
R		
A	Limiting Action	Decisive Action
L	Limiting Language	Decisive Language
T	Limiting Thinking	No Limit Thinking

Years ago, Loral was walking through a hotel lobby with Mark Victor Hanson, co-author of the Chicken Soup For The Soul series. As they walked, Mark looked at Loral and said, "There are more opportunities in one day that come into my life than I can do for the rest of my life."

Loral remembers thinking, "Wow! I can't wait until that happens to me. That would be great." At that point, all she could see were walls and obstacles slowing her down and keeping her from reaching her goals. Her thinking was limited. In fact, she had been aware of her limiting thinking for years and years.

Loral worked to eliminate her limited thinking and she became a millionaire by age 34. Now that she is so successful, it's even clearer to her that she has no room for limited thinking; it can only hold her back. Instead of limits, Loral's life is filled with many lucrative joint ventures, collaborations and fabulous relationships, which make her life more stimulating, rewarding and fun!

DECISIVE LANGUAGE = DECISIVE ACTION

DECISIVE ACTION = EXPANSIVE RESULTS

When you commit yourself to decisive thinking, you'll start to speak decisively and use decisive language. Decisive language breeds decisive action, which creates expansive results.

"That's interesting, Loral," you might say, "but how do I use this on a day-to-day basis?" Here's how:

- ➤ Get that T-Chart from the previous page to remind you of the financial messages you want to atrophy, as well as those you want to strengthen.
- ➤ Focus on what you want to create, as opposed to what you no longer want.
- ➤ Constantly monitor your language throughout the day. Listen to your words; pay attention and hear exactly what you say.

> ➢ List the limiting language you use on a regular basis.
> ➢ Eliminate that negative language by replacing your limiting language with decisive language.

Remember, the word "if" is limiting, but the word "when" is decisive. "I will," "I won't," "Yes," and "No" are decisive. "Can" and "Can't" are about capability and have nothing to do with decisiveness. Decisiveness means that you will or you won't; it's not evasive or hard to pin down. It shows that you made a choice.

Decisive language introduces decisive actions.

When you commit to achieving your goal with integrity, you will find yourself using decisive language. By speaking decisively, you commit to yourself, your actions and your team. You assert that you will do what it takes by a certain time.

Certainly decisive language makes things happen; it expresses your clarity. Decisive language convinces and intrigues others. Decisiveness creates trust and confidence in your team. Decisiveness creates consistency and certainty in commanding your resources. When you use decisive language, you lay the groundwork for decisive action to begin. Expansive results will emerge in your bank account and in your whole life.

GUERRILLA TACTIC

After you've listed the limiting language you use, share your list with three or four close and supportive people. Tell them to stop you whenever you use limiting language. Instruct them to interrupt you on the spot, even if it's right in the middle of a conversation.

As you use more decisive language, you'll act more decisively. Implement a monthly Money Day, a day when you spend time on your finances. Schedule it on your calendar. On Money Day, clean up your paper work, file papers, pay bills, put your financials online, review your assets and liabilities, and check your credit card and investment accounts. Research and explore new investments, lower interest rates or joint ventures.

Wealthy people devote at least a day each week to attending to their finances, so once a month should be a snap for you. A monthly Money Day will help you plan and keep on top of your finances. It will help you anticipate problems and give you time to avoid or minimize them. It can help eliminate those last-minute panics when you don't have enough to pay all your bills.

We would like to leave you with a final question. When you think about becoming wealthy, what does that mean to you? Think about all of the ramifications. Then identify your definition of "wealthy" and what it means to you. Do you define wealthy as being a millionaire or a multi-millionaire? Is it amassing a hundred million dollars? How would you spend or use that money?

Your Financial Conditioning: Your Personal Money Psychology

Before we leave this chapter, we want to give you one more exercise. This exercise will challenge you to the core and reinforce everything that we've covered up to this point in this chapter.

Take out your wallet and count your cash. If you fall into the traditional pattern you will carry $30 to $40 in cash if you are a woman, and $70 to $100 if you are a man. Now comes the big test: carry more cash than you've ever carried for the next thirty days. For example, a hundred-dollar bill, five hundred-dollar bills or whatever amount feels like a stretch to you. Choose whatever amount makes you uncomfortable to carry in your wallet.

Stretching will make you more aware of your financial conditioning. We want you to feel a little tension in your money muscles, break some of your long-standing rules and try something new. It might feel a little uncomfortable to carry so much money, but it will start to change your thinking. It will help you think in terms of prosperity (the prosperity mindset), the abundance of money and how you feel with so much cash in your pocket. It will also help you focus on the wealth you really want to create.

Execute the following written commitment. Date it, sign it and place it prominently where you can see it every day.

AGREEMENT

I hereby agree that I, _____
(your name), will carry at all times on my person no
less than $ _____ (the amount) from today
_____ (today's date) until
_____ (30 days). I will carry
such sum in order to examine my feelings about money.

_____   _____
Date   Your Signature

Now, let's return to the example T-chart on page 33. List the messages you want to strengthen on a sticky note and put it on the cash in your wallet. Every time you think about spending cash or when you need some reinforcement about the wealth you're going to create, the note will remind you of your goal and support the beliefs and money muscles you want to grow.

At the end of the 30-day period, write on a separate sheet how carrying additional cash made you feel and how it changed your outlook toward money. Keep that sheet and refer to it from time to time and on Money Days.

Your Financial Conditioning: Your Personal Money Psychology

SUCCESS STORIES

Paul Rakofsky

"As a CPA for 25 years, I made an excellent income and achieved my primary goals. Then I asked, 'What next?' I realized that the next step in accounting wasn't what I wanted, so I stepped away with no income and none on the horizon.

When I met Loral, I decided to jump on board with her in real estate. I had been living off my credit cards and earning no cash income. I knew I needed to do things differently, to change how I thought about wealth and to make some dramatic shifts in what I was doing to accumulate wealth.

Now, almost two years later, my life has completely changed. I am confident. I know that by following the steps Loral recommends, I will create wealth. It's a different way of thinking and I'm no longer hampered by doubts about what is possible.

I have invested in three real estate properties and have about $75,000 in equity. I couldn't have done this without taking the first step of creating a shift in how I thought about my life as a business. I'd lost self-confidence, and lost satisfaction working with accounting clients. When I understood that my life was a business and that being a CPA was the cash machine that would enable me to invest effectively in real estate, I was ready to work with different people. About that time, Loral approached me to help people with their baselines and forecasts - their wealth measurement systems - and some tax preparation and planning.

Now that I am using my skills and talents to work with people who are like-minded about building wealth, I have the confidence to approach other areas of my life more easily. I have no problem standing in front of a room full of people to present wealth-building concepts, and I'm not hesitant to work with my team to buy more real estate properties. I have the certainty and confidence that I do have something important to contribute and what I contribute has significant value."

Sid Smith

"At the end of 2003, after spending three years struggling to keep my coaching business afloat, I was beginning to live off my credit cards. I found it nearly impossible to create financial forecasts on the basis of anything other than guesswork and prayers. I knew I had to change, but I didn't know what or how to change!

Loral lit the fuse that ignited the bomb that exploded my world. She helped me see that I was too emotionally involved in being a coach, and that I'd lost sight that coaching was my business. She said, 'Your cash machine isn't coaching, it's writing.'

It took the first 120 days of my 120-day plan to wrap my mind, emotions, and ego around this new concept of making money. I had to let go of the concept of myself as a coach and embrace the idea that my business existed primarily to make money. That didn't mean that I couldn't love what I was doing, but if I wasn't making any money, then the business wasn't serving me.

I'm now in my second 120-day plan, which is about building my business. It includes marketing and promoting myself as a writer, as well as establishing systems and structures that will enable my business to become more profitable over time. I've changed how I think about my business and myself. I've learned to separate who I am personally, from who I am professionally and what I do for money. The process has been miraculous. As soon as I understood how much I had been blocking my own success, the gates opened. Within weeks my client base had grown to capacity and I've been raising my rates monthly. Changing from focusing on my emotional needs to my financial and business goals opened the doors to new business opportunities and each new opportunity has led to more referrals.

As my business grows, I've learned how to manage my energy more efficiently. Running my life as a business means being extremely practical and pragmatic about my time. I've dropped some friends and met a few new ones. I partition my time, which includes turning the phone and email off when I'm writing. It also means taking breaks to take care of my body and spirit. I'm realizing that it's all possible - wealth, health, and happiness - and I'm enjoying being successful."

SUMMING UP

Don't expect a million dollars or more to land in your personal bank account. Even if it does, the government will take most of it in taxes. We also don't believe that God would deliver a million dollars to chaos. So, let's start to change your psychology about money and work on conditioning you to become wealthy. This will help you build the foundation that will make your dreams come true. Remember . . . what you think about, you create. We want you in a positive, pro-active conversation, driven by a healthy relationship to money.

LORAL'S LEARNING LOOP

What are three things you learned from this chapter?

_____

_____

_____

_____

_____

_____

_____

_____

_____

What three actions will you take as a result of this chapter?

_____

_____

_____

_____

_____

_____

List the dates when you will begin and complete your three actions.

_____

_____

_____

To whom will you be accountable?

_____

_____

Section II

YOUR
WEALTH
FOUNDATION

3

Your Financial Baseline

*"Until a person commits to the first step,
the next step cannot appear."*

Now that you've learned how to clear out your mind and clean up your financial vocabulary, it's time to get a handle on your current financial picture. This is a point where many people simply stall out. And little wonder! Most people don't know what documents to keep or how to organize them, so they do nothing. Worse, they don't know how to use the information in the documents they have to make it easier to achieve wealth faster. This is a key distinction between guerrilla wealth tactics and the Industrial Age model. We're moving decisively away from the old budgeting model, which was just dividing your money to meet expenses as best you could. Worse, as a concept, budgeting is deeply rooted in the scarcity mindset of skimping.

Now you're going to start living your life in a truly businesslike and professional way, which positions you to build wealth. To do that, we need to know where you stand financially now.

In the Information Age model, we start with something that looks familiar - organizing financial papers - but then use the information in those papers to create a personal Profit and Loss Statement and a Balance Sheet. This provides the more useful Financial Baseline, which is foundational to the guerrilla tactics we'll be covering throughout the book.

Your Financial Baseline

Before you decide to ignore this step - and we know there's a big temptation to do that - you need to have a good reason to do it. An example will help.

Imagine if you parachuted from a plane into the middle of a desert. All you can see for miles and miles is emptiness, sand and blinding sun. Your goal is to get to Lincoln, Nebraska. How would you start? Which way would you go? It would be absolutely critical to your success, and in this case, your life, that you first establish exactly where you've landed. Then, and only then, could you head in the right direction to get to Lincoln.

When you don't know where you are, there's no way to know what direction to take. No matter which way you go, you're guessing. It's easy to get lost. You might get lucky and make all the right turns the first time, but would you really want to leave it to chance? We don't think so.

The exact same thing is true about your financial success. You must start with an accurate reading of where you are financially; you must take inventory. This is your "financial baseline." Think of your financial baseline as a blueprint or financial fingerprint that you can glance at to immediately see your financial condition. Once you know your financial baseline, you can get control of your money in a meaningful way. Only then can you begin growing your wealth and designing the life you want.

We've learned in coaching others that this step has almost instant rewards for people. First, they relax - maybe for the first time in years. Even if their financial

Your Financial Baseline

lives are in a shambles, just knowing the truth of it is a relief. If you're currently in debt or your expenses just seem to spiral out of control, not looking at your financial picture actually makes you feel worse, not better. Not knowing is a constant, under-the-radar stress you simply don't need in your life.

An unexpected surprise for many people is an almost automatic "course correction" that takes place when they see where they are and where their money is going. Many people are unconscious of the "leaks" in their money. Often just seeing it on paper gets them into action. "We spend how much on lattes every week?"

Another reward is a great sense of control. Suddenly you're no longer just drifting along. There's tremendous motivation in knowing you're beginning to model the behavior of the wealthy. Quite simply, one of their greatest tactics is being aware of where the money goes.

Be encouraged. Getting it all together the first time won't be nearly as hard as you imagine. And it truly will mark the turning point from "scraping by," "getting along," "doing pretty well" or even "doing better than most" to a well-charted course toward financial freedom.

Your Financial Baseline

You can determine your financial baseline in three steps:

1. Organize Your Financial Filing Cabinet.

2. Complete Your Personal/Business Profit and Loss Statements.

3. Complete Your Personal/Business Balance Sheets.

YOUR FINANCIAL FILING CABINET

"First comes thought;
then organization of that thought,
into ideas and plans;
then transformation of those plans into reality.
The beginning, as you will observe,
is in your imagination."

Napoleon Hill

Relax. If your financial papers, unopened mail, bills, receipts and statements are scattered throughout the house, stuffed in drawers or shoeboxes, you're not alone. For most people that's perfectly normal. But it's not normal for the wealthy. And since the whole point of this book is to propel you toward wealth, we're going to make this essential step as easy and painless as possible for you.

Since, despite your hopes, it never seems to miraculously organize itself, roll up your sleeves and let's begin the process of building your financial filing cabinet.

Your Financial Baseline

Let's begin by collecting all of your papers. You may have to search through your desk and open all those unopened envelopes filled with statements.

Once you dig them out, spread them across the floor or across the dining room table. These pieces of paper may be highly charged emotionally. Some may remind you that you made some foolish impulse purchases. Others may be evidence of your casual attitude toward reconciling your checking account.

Stop!

Disengage emotionally now. These are just pieces of paper you want to sort. If you let them, they'll make you feel so awful or so overwhelmed, you'll stop. It's possible that your past dealings with money just brings up too much guilt or remorse, if for no other reason than you haven't been as sharp about money as you could have been. So, if you need to, take a minute to remind yourself, "That was then; this is now," and you're taking control responsibly.

The first part of this exercise is as easy as an elementary school game. Just divide all the papers into stacks with others like them. Here are the categories:

Banking Records
> Checking
> Savings
> Bankbooks
> Banking statements
> Certificates
> Safe deposit box key
> Cash receipts

Your Financial Baseline

Bills, Payables, Expenses
- Credit card statements
- Utility
- Phone
- Internet
- Cable
- Gardener

Legal Documents
- Powers of attorney
- Financial agreements
- Partnership agreements
- Living will
- Do-not-resuscitate order
- Will
- Trust agreements

Insurance Policies
- Life
- Health
- Disability
- Business continuation
- Homeowner's/Renter's
- Auto
- Employee benefit data

Group Insurance
- Pension plan
- Savings/profit sharing

Your Financial Baseline

Investment Records
- ➤ Profit and loss statements
- ➤ Balance sheets
- ➤ Investment statements
- ➤ Buy and sell documents
- ➤ Stock certificates
- ➤ Bond certificates
- ➤ College education funds

Income Tax Records
- ➤ Current year backup
- ➤ Past years' records
- ➤ Yearly worksheets

Housing Records
- ➤ Improvements
- ➤ Property tax payments
- ➤ Mortgage payments
- ➤ Appliance warranties
- ➤ Repair and maintenance receipts

General Documents
- ➤ Birth certificates
- ➤ Marriage certificate
- ➤ Adoption records
- ➤ Social Security cards
- ➤ Divorce decree
- ➤ Passport

GUERRILLA INTELLIGENCE

Store the original copies of important documents such as wills, trusts, deeds and stock certificates in a safe, fireproof box or a bank safe deposit box. Make copies of each of those documents and place them in your financial filing cabinet. Inform key people in your life where the originals can be found.

Photocopy both sides of all of your credit, identification and membership cards and keep them in your safe deposit box, safe or fire-proof box, and in your financial filing cabinet. Do the same with the personal-information page of your passport and all vaccination certificates. When you travel, take a copy with you and give another copy to someone you trust at home.

By the way, you can receive copies of any of the forms in this book for your individual use. To request them, just email info@liveoutloud.com and give us your email address or phone number. We'll be happy to send them to you electronically.

So now that you have all of your documents in nice neat little piles, it is time for you to file them away!

CREATE A SYSTEM

In the beginning, you'll have to organize and create the structure for your financial filing cabinet, so set up a system that's easy and intuitive to use. Create a system that's simple for you. Otherwise you won't be able to find information you need quickly.

In time, you'll have the ability to hire others to keep your system in order. You can employ bookkeepers or assistants who specialize in doing this precise work. Often, they're experts who know shortcuts and can give you time-saving tips. One thing we do caution you about is that when you work with bookkeepers, accountants or others, have them adopt your system. Don't feel obligated to adopt their systems or purchase a complex organizing system at the office supply store. It's no smarter to have a complicated, unworkable system than leaving your papers in a mess. Make it simple.

Here is an example of a simple financial filing cabinet:

➤ Create a filing system to track all of your monthly income and expenses. Set up individual files for each of your financial categories. For example,

- Income—Make a separate file for your income documents. Include papers, receipts and other information on your wages and all investment income such as interest, dividends and royalties.

Your Financial Baseline

- Expenses—Create individual files for each of your personal payables, such as bills and receipts for your telephone, utilities, rent, credit card statements, etc.
➢ Separate your insurance policies and place everything except your health and medical policies in one file. Organize them by date.
➢ Place all of your health and medical insurance policies, bills and information in a file. In this file, also store your legal health documents, such as living wills, durable powers of attorney and "do-not-resuscitate" orders. In addition, include papers from your gym and exercise programs and instructions.
➢ Place your assets and portfolio accounts in separate files so you can easily review each of them. Place like investments together; for example, keep all of your real estate papers together and all of your stocks and bonds together.
➢ File all legal documents relating to business together. Included could be papers regarding any legal entities you use, such as certificates of incorporation, partnership agreements and fictitious name certificates.
➢ Open another file for your personal and family legal matters. It can include your will, powers of attorney (other than health and medical), trusts and estate planning documents.

The guide outlined previously will help you categorize important materials. You should also make a master list (in print, on your computer or both) that identifies each document, all account numbers and where originals are located. Once you've completed this exercise, give a copy to your spouse, partner, a trusted friend, a family member, your attorney and/or accountant or other advisors.

PROFIT AND LOSS STATEMENTS

When you track your income and expenses every month, you can instantly see your progress and know whether you're making or losing money. Profit and Loss Statements, which are also known as "income statements," pinpoint where you're doing well and where adjustments are needed. They'll help you plan for growth, expansion and future investments. For example, just one glance can tell you the ideal time to buy more stocks or real estate . . . or to grow your business.

Profit and Loss (P&L) Statements should list all of the income you earn and all of the expenses you incur (right down to the last latte and pair of shoes) each month.

If yours is a two-income family, list both partners' incomes and expenses separately because you may be liable for, or impacted by, your partner's finances.

You should also do a P&L for both your business and your personal worlds. As we move through this book, you'll learn why it's essential that you keep them separate. We'll also give you more details on how your business can absorb expenses, which you may now be paying from your personal funds, that are actually valid business expenses/deductions.

GUERRILLA WEALTH

Your Financial Baseline

Personal Profit and Loss Statement

INCOME		EXPENSE	
Item	Amount	Item	Amount
Earned			
		Tax	
Passive			
Total		Total	
	Income - Expenses = $ Cashflow		

Your Financial Baseline

Business Profit and Loss Statement

INCOME		EXPENSE	
Item	Amount	Item	Amount
Earned			
		Tax	
Passive			
Total		Total	
	Income - Expenses = $ Cashflow		

Your Financial Baseline

When you create monthly P&L Statements, you always know your current financial condition. Therefore, you can move decisively and promptly to jump on opportunities before your competitors even know they exist.

GUERRILLA TACTIC

If your business and personal expenses (and income) are commingled and you use one account for both, immediately open a business account. To open a business account, you must show the bank the following:

A. Business license.
B. Fictitious name certificate or Articles of Incorporation or Organization.

Call your bank and they'll tell you exactly what they need. The necessary documents are easily obtainable from your local city or county government, so contact them for specific information. Since laws differ from place to place, call ahead to learn exactly where you should go, what information you must provide and how much it will cost. If you operate more than one business, you'll need to produce copies of each company's business documents to open separate bank accounts.

Your Financial Baseline

P & L TIPS

On your personal and business P&L statements:

➢ Be extremely detailed. Include all of your income and expenses, regardless of the size, so your statement provides your complete financial picture.

➢ In the income column, list earned income and passive income. Passive income is what you earn from investments. If your income fluctuates from month to month, list the average for the last 90 days in the income column. If it varies wildly, then use the average for the past six months.

It's important to identify how much of your income you earn and how much comes in passively. Passive income is essential for wealth creation and is generated by investing your assets well.

➢ In the expense column, first list all taxes you've paid. If you're an employee, the amount you were taxed will be listed on your paycheck stub. If you're a business owner, file quarterly income tax estimates.

➢ The amount in your income column should balance with that in the expense column. What you're left with is the bottom line, your profit or loss, your cash flow.

Your Financial Baseline

➤ Calculate all business expenses that you currently pay from your personal account and adjust them accordingly. Separate your personal and business expenses and allocate each to the appropriate account. Some of your business expenses might be:

  ➤ Rent (office or home office deduction)
  ➤ Utilities
  ➤ Phone
  ➤ Legal fees
  ➤ Entertainment
  ➤ Gifts
  ➤ Staff
  ➤ Meals
  ➤ Travel
  ➤ Automobile
  ➤ Gas
  ➤ Insurance
  ➤ Office supplies
  ➤ Computer equipment
  ➤ Education
  ➤ Accounting/bookkeeping fees
  ➤ Hiring family members to work in the business

➤ If you have a life insurance policy, list the premium costs in the expense column. Conversely, list the policy's cash values in the asset column.

GUERRILLA INTELLIGENCE

Isn't it curious that we've been conditioned to call the money that's left over after we've paid all of our bills "disposable income."

What does that mean, that we should throw it away? Why is it disposable?

Would we spend it any differently if it were called "cash flow?" We believe that you would.

In preparing P&L statements, don't guess or enter what you think it "should be." List precisely how you've been making and spending your money so that you get a true picture of your financial life. Later, we'll discuss forecasting, which is designing a plan to reach what you want to achieve based on where you are currently.

After you complete your personal and business P&L statements, share them with your accountability partner, your coach and your wealth team. Solicit their opinions and input because it will deepen your understanding about your finances and improve your bottom line.

BALANCE SHEETS

Your personal balance sheet reveals your net worth; it reflects your past financial habits. It's a complete and comprehensive review of your entire financial picture. A balance sheet must include everything you own - your assets and everything you owe - your liabilities. If anything is left out, you won't get the complete picture.

If you own a business, you'll also need a balance sheet for each of your businesses. On your business balance sheet, remember to include shareholder equity, office equipment, lines of credit, loans that were used to start your business, good will, etc.

As you create your balance sheets, examine the lifestyle choices you've made to this point in your life. Look specifically at your bank statements, your credit card statements and your cash receipts from the last ninety days. Examine your monetary trail, because it will be your financial report card. How do you feel? What do you see? Is your financial life aligned to your values?

GUERRILLA WEALTH

Your Financial Baseline

Personal Balance Sheet

ASSETS		LIABILITIES	
Item	Amount	Item	Amount
Total		Total	
	Assets - Liabilities = $ Net Worth		

GUERRILLA WEALTH

Your Financial Baseline

Business Balance Sheet

ASSETS		LIABILITIES	
Item	Amount	Item	Amount
Total		Total	
	Assets - Liabilities = $ Net Worth		

GUERRILLA INTELLIGENCE

Tactically, preparing Profit and Loss Statements or Balance Sheets should have nothing to do with emotions; emotional feelings should not be a part of the equation. Preparing a Profit and Loss Statement or a Balance Sheet should be an exercise based purely on documented facts.

Unfortunately, 90 percent of all financial decisions are emotionally driven because people have not calculated their financial baselines. As a result, they make monetary decisions on the basis of their feelings, not on facts. Money - those little, green, paper notes that we all try to acquire - only drives emotions when we give it significance. In other words, it's our conditioning about money that provides it with emotional significance. So don't let your feelings cloud your financial judgment.

Your Financial Baseline

BALANCE SHEET TIPS

> ➤ In preparing the asset column of your balance sheet, list everything you own. Even list those assets that are producing a negative cash flow. For example, when you own real estate and it's not providing a positive cash flow, list (1) how much equity you have in the property in the asset column, (2) the mortgage amount on the liability side and (3) the amount of negative cash flow in the income column.
>
>> • Contrary to popular belief, when you list your home, enter the amount of your equity in your home in the asset column and the outstanding mortgage balance in the liability column.
>
> ➤ In the liability column, list the total amount of each of your liabilities independently. In other words, list what you owe on each of your credit cards (MasterCard®, Visa®, CitiBank®, American Express® and so on) and your total credit-card debt. Separate each of your utility payments. If you have more than one student loan, list each of them separately. Also list all of your consumer debt, such as credit cards and loans, separately because you will need that precise information to eliminate your debt.
>
> ➤ In the liability column, learn what constitutes good and bad debt. Good debt is attached to an asset, and you will acquire good debt as you grow wealthy. For example:

Your Financial Baseline

- If you own a parcel of real estate worth $100,000, but owe $90,000, the $90,000 is good debt because the land should increase in value. Therefore, you probably won't want to pay off the debt.
- Bad debt is consumer debt, such as credit cards. It's debt attached to your lifestyle choices. Since your new Manolos, DVD player or dinner at Chez Chic that you charged won't increase in value, the interest payment you incurred is considered bad debt.

➤ Subtract the total amount of your liabilities from the total amount of your assets to determine your net worth.

EXAMPLE 3-5

Total Assets	$730,000
Total Liabilities	$360,000
Net Worth	$370,000

Remember, your balance sheet is the sum of all that you own and everything you owe!

CONGRATULATIONS

Congratulations on your good work!

You've cleaned up your financial mess and now have a financial filing cabinet that's in order. You've also completed your personal and business Profit and Loss Statements and Balance Sheets. By doing so, you've taken the most important steps in determining your financial baseline and moving yourself in new directions. Not only did you find out how much you're worth, but you also learned where your assets and liabilities lie, which will be advantageous when opportunities arise and you must act quickly. When you know your financial baseline, you'll also know which assets you can quickly sell to maximize your opportunities. Those assets may have been losing money or not making as much as other investments that you want to retain.

Completing your P&L Statements and Balance Sheets are the most intense and critical steps in your wealth building process. However, they'll also make it far easier when you have to fill out detailed credit applications. You've now completed the hardest, most demanding work, but it was entirely necessary to position you to create your wealth.

Understanding your financial baseline will be a relief. And many people, especially women, are amazed by how much they're actually worth. Knowing what you're worth will change your life.

We can't encourage you enough to maintain your

Your Financial Baseline

financial baseline month after month. It's going to take some work, effort and reconditioning, but if you want to be wealthy, it's the only way to go. Your financial situation will be your guiding light. Knowing your financial status will give you calm confidence. It will teach you how to look at financial numbers and make educated decisions.

In the space provided, list your observations on completing your P&L Statements and Balance Sheets.

1. How difficult was it to complete them and why?

_____

_____

_____

_____

_____

_____

2. How emotional was it to complete them?

_____

_____

_____

_____

_____

_____

Your Financial Baseline

3. What value did your receive by completing them?

_____

_____

_____

_____

_____

_____

4. How helpful do you expect this tool to be and why?

_____

_____

_____

_____

_____

_____

How much extra money (cash flow) do you have each month both personally and in your business?

Business _____   Personal _____

What is your personal net worth? _____

Your Financial Baseline

SUCCESS STORY

Connie Becerril

"I was working 10-12 hours per day in the accounting business when the company suddenly shut down. I had no plan and no job, so I decided to try real estate. I started by determining my financial baseline and determined the amounts of my assets and liabilities. Then, I figured out how much income I would need on a monthly basis in order to live the way I wanted.

When I laid it all out, I realized I could get immediate cash flow by building a mother-in-law apartment in my house. So I built it and brought in my first passive income. Since then, I've purchased three other houses - all without spending a dime of my own money. By using other people's money, I spent a couple of months this summer 'working' in Europe. I set it up so that income came in regularly regardless of whatever else I was doing. Establishing my financial baseline was key because without it, I would not have known how easy it was to make my way without a job.

Having a financial baseline also gives me the freedom to develop future plans. I know where I am and can figure out where I'm going. I've found a partner in DC. Although he's never invested in real estate, I'm confident that with his good credit, we'll have no problem closing the deal. I am also buying land in Italy to develop a time-share condominium.

I'm a different person from who I was a year ago. I love learning about asset allocation, entity structuring, and developing my cash machine. Making money is fun. I'm in the process of creating a Web site that will generate cash by integrating what I've learned about real estate into a system that will benefit realtors, lenders, and people selling their own homes. The net effect of all this has been creating cash flow and tripling my net worth in less than 120 days. As I develop my cash machine and begin getting commissions from the Website and from leading seminars, I will continue to review my baseline to understand where I am and plan where I'm going. The idea is to create your baseline and then just go do it. That's what gives you the confidence to create wealth."

SUMMING UP

When you know your financial baseline, you'll have a clear picture of your current monetary position, which will help you plan and make necessary changes. Maintain your financial filing cabinet and prepare Profit and Loss Statements and Balance Sheets on a consistent basis. Hire a bookkeeper or keep financially current by yourself; it's up to you. But, either way, keep current. Make it a regular part of your routine. Remember, if you don't know where you are, you'll never get where you want to go.

LORAL'S LEARNING LOOP

What are three things you learned from this chapter?

_____

_____

_____

_____

_____

_____

What three actions will you take as a result of this chapter?

_____

_____

_____

_____

_____

_____

List the dates when you will begin and complete your three actions.

_____

_____

_____

Your Financial Baseline

To whom will you be accountable?

_____

_____

4

Your Financial Freedom Day

*"There's simply nothing else like knowing
you can plan for and reach your own
personal Financial Freedom Day."*

Here comes the good part! Planning for your
Financial Freedom Day!

Once again, we developed this concept for the
Information Age. Here's why it's so revolutionary: in
the Industrial Age model, as we've discussed, you saved
as best you could for your own retirement fund. You
also had some security with a company, so there was a
predictable pension waiting for you after the retirement
party. Of course, you also had Social Security.

Welcome to the new reality of the Information Age.
Life-long jobs with company pensions are relics of the
past. Creating a reasonable retirement fund can still
be a hassle, as many Baby Boomers are discovering.
Social Security is anything but secure. This strikes fear
into the hearts of people who are clinging stubbornly
to the old model of working and retiring, hoping it'll
all work out.

By comparison, the Information Age model is
actually quite liberating and can relieve your anxiety
and uncertainty. Conceptually, you have to embrace
the notion that you're in charge of your own income
and financial future. You can't look to companies or
the government to give you security. You're responsible
for your finances now. You'll be responsible in the
future.

Your Financial Freedom Day

Financial Freedom Day isn't about having the money you need ready on the day of your retirement. Retirement is an Industrial Age idea. Following guerrilla wealth tactics, you can chart your course to peg your Financial Freedom Day much sooner than traditional retirement and enjoy your life more fully at a much earlier date. If the dot.com era taught us anything, it was that young people have the capacity to reach millionaire status, even if lack of experience prevented many of them from leveraging their wealth to survive the crash with their money intact.

Your Financial Freedom Day is the time you've always dreamed of when you finally are free to do what you really want, as opposed to what you must. We like to say that it's when you get to lead the "want to" life instead of the "have to" life. Instead of having to go to work to pay the bills, you can sit back, relax and enjoy life as your assets work for you.

Your Financial Freedom Day can be the most exciting, satisfying and rewarding day of your life, and working toward it can be exhilarating. It's the day when you can say with all certainty that you have a CHOICE. Do you love your work? Keep working. Want to try something else? Why not? Isn't that an empowering feeling?

To get to your Financial Freedom Day, there's still more to do. In most cases, a gap exists between where you are now - Your Financial Baseline - and where you hope to be - Your Financial Freedom Day. The next step is to figure out the size of the gap and how to bridge it.

Your Financial Freedom Day

When you know where you're going, it's easier to plan action, to map out the route, and to find the quickest, most direct road to obtain what you seek. It'll also help you to identify potential obstacles in your path so you can avoid them or reduce their impact. Knowing that your efforts can set you free is a great motivator to keep you on track.

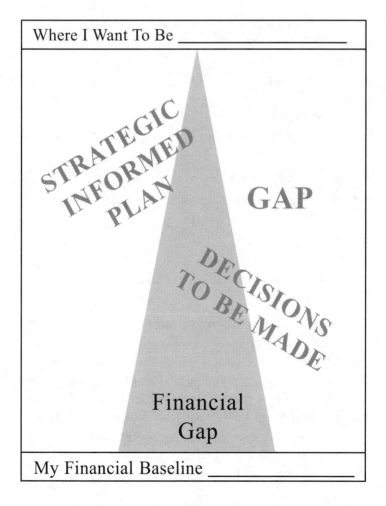

Where I Want To Be _____

STRATEGIC INFORMED PLAN

GAP

DECISIONS TO BE MADE

Financial Gap

My Financial Baseline _____

Your Financial Freedom Day

In the chart outlined on the previous page, you've already created your financial baseline. You can use that to choose your Financial Freedom Day. To declare your Financial Freedom Day, you need to determine:

1.   How much money (cash flow) do you want to receive each month? _____

2.   What do you want your net worth to be? _____

3.   By what age? _____

4.   By what day, month and year? _____

Now that you have declared your Financial Freedom Day, let's begin to bridge the gap by forming your clear vision and specific goals.

CLEAR VISION

Few people create wealth simply to be "rich," they usually have other motives. Wealth is the vehicle that gives them the means to do what they want. It's also a byproduct that comes from something deep and powerful, such as their ambition, curiosity, dedication, passion and hard work. We truly believe that money isn't the most important objective, but it has the greatest impact. It allows people the means to realize their dreams—their vision.

Your Financial Freedom Day

People who lack clear vision are like rudderless ships; they wander aimlessly, never knowing whether they're on course. They may reach a goal without recognizing it, and change direction. Although most people have some idea of what they want, few have a clear and compelling vision of wealth.

This vision keeps you on course. It helps you maintain your focus. Your vision must be powerful. It should make you want to jump out of bed in the morning and energize you throughout the day to work toward reaching your dreams.

It helps when your vision has a strong emotional component, such as passion or a burning desire to reach your goals. Emotions fuel your quests. They provide the power that drives you closer to your objectives. When your clear vision is emotionally motivated, you eagerly commit to the journey.

Visions can be complex and come in all different sizes and shapes. As part of their vision, most wealthy people utilize multiple income vehicles, such as corporations, partnerships, trusts and foundations. Their streams of income can include real estate, stock market investments, art, antiques and other collectables. Much of their diversity is attributable to the fact that they spend lots of time devising strategies and dreaming up ways to accelerate their wealth. They constantly come up with new visions for creating additional wealth.

A wonderful definition of vision appeared in Cynthia D. Scott and Dennis T. Jaffe's book, Organizational Vision, Values and Mission (Crisp

Publications, 1993). They wrote:

> "A vision is a picture of a preferred future state, a description of what it would be like to be some years from now. It is a dynamic picture of the future. It is more than a dream or set of hopes; it is a commitment. The vision provides the context for designing or managing the changes that will be necessary to reach those goals."

So what's your reason for wanting to accumulate wealth? What's your compelling vision?

- ➢ Do you want to provide a service to the world?
- ➢ Do you hope to build a legacy for your family?
- ➢ Do you have philanthropic goals?
- ➢ Do you simply want a life of ease and luxury for yourself?

Your vision must be greater than just quitting your job. Visions become more powerful when they're consistent with, or products of, your values. When you truly believe in the objectives you're pursuing, it's easier to work toward your goal. You can work longer and harder, and have more fun. You can be more fulfilled and more successful. For example, if you're deeply committed to nature, you'll be more likely to reap greater rewards from working on outdoor projects than those that keep you stuck inside.

Think about and identify your values. What are they? What makes you feel passionate? Look back on situations in which you had fun, and were happy, successful, proud, satisfied and made money. What did you like most about them and what would you like to replicate? Similarly, what type of environment turns you on? Do you like stability, working under pressure, heated competition or living on the edge? When you identify your values, you'll be happier and more successful pursuing objectives that are consistent with those values.

GUERRILLA INTELLIGENCE

The insurance industry's actuarial tables tell us that those people whose goal is to retire at age 65 usually do so. But interestingly, when retiring at 65 is their sole goal, most of them pass away within two years. Why? The answer is because they haven't bothered to plan their life beyond that point.

The dictionary defines the word "retire" as: "to withdraw from action, retreat." It's also a synonym for going to bed, which is exactly what so many retired folks do; they withdraw, remove themselves from life and become reclusive. To some extent, they withdraw because they have to - they simply don't have enough money to live big lives and they rely on the government to subsidize their golden years.

The purpose of this book is to show you how to design your life for your Financial Freedom Day. By doing so, you can enjoy your "want to" life as opposed to living a "have to" life. This requires vision, focus and commitment.

SET FINANCIAL GOALS

Now that you have your vision, it's time to set your financial goals. Before you begin to set your goals, we want to warn you that numbers, any numbers, can be discouraging. They can scare people away and make them abandon their long-time dreams. Understand that what you may initially see as problems could turn out to be lessons or opportunities. Consider the numbers you come up with as reference points or measurement devices, rather than roadblocks.

We also want to share with you that Goal Setting is not a random thing. In order to be successful, goals must be set with careful attention to detail. Start by identifying your most short-term, realistic goals and begin to work with them. Think of these goals as starting points, places where you must begin, and realize that they can always be changed or adjusted, especially as you begin to achieve more.

Below is a chart that explains how we feel goals should be set in order to achieve the optimum results.

SMART GOALS

Set SMART goals. SMART goals are:

S = SPECIFIC

They contain the complete details of everything you set out to accomplish. They state exactly what you want and provide a step-by-step plan, laying out the methods you'll use to get it.

Your Financial Freedom Day

M = MEASURABLE

They include identifiable milestones such as dates, specific achievements and dollar amounts to measure both your progress and your success. For example, the number of new clients you land each month, how much money you deposit in your account or the amount of investment capital you raise.

A = ACHIEVABLE

This refers to external economic forces and the current market. Achievable goals are attainable, or capable of being accomplished, given the current trends, and even the economic climate. For example, in real estate, mini-storage units may be hot at one point, but not a good choice when demand cools. Consider the specific external factors that may affect your investing plans.

R = REALISTIC

This refers to internal factors that affect your ability to succeed. These include your character, perseverance and willingness to spend the necessary time to gain expertise and pursue your wealth objectives. Write down what you must do to reach each goal. You must be able to achieve that goal by using the tools at your disposal or those you can acquire. Find a mentor who's doing a bigger and better job with a larger company. Mentors can provide reality checks by telling you about their journey, the path they took and what is involved to get there.

T = TIMELY

Each goal must contain benchmarks and deadlines that you must meet at various stages until the goal is reached. Timelines will keep you on track and on schedule, and create a sense of urgency to keep you motivated.

Now that you know how to set SMART GOALS, let's begin on yours. What are your financial goals? First, list them generally. Do you want to start your own business, save for your retirement or build an investment account? Begin by identifying your broad objectives, then zero in on and describe your goals in greater detail.

Exactly how much money do you need to make?

What other financial plateaus would you like to reach?

For example, I want to have a net worth of over $10 million and an annual income of $1 million; to own homes in San Francisco, Paris, Barcelona and Maine; to start a children's magazine on how to become wealthy; and to contribute at least $300,000 to my favorite charities each year.

List your specific goals below.

1. _____

2. _____

3. _____

Your Financial Freedom Day

Are you sure they're big enough? Will they satisfy you in 10, 20 or 30 years? Why don't you crank your financial goals up higher and really reach for your dreams? But be realistic. Remember you can adjust, change and expand as you grow.

GUERRILLA TACTIC

Let's get real. We want you to have your Financial Freedom Day just as much as you want to achieve it. What we know after years of coaching and mentoring is that the ultimate Freedom Day comes from passive income to support your lifestyle. There are three Financial Freedom Day benchmarks that you must achieve along the way:

1. Get your earned income to be greater than your expenses.

2. Get out of consumer debt.

3. Consistently put money into your wealth account and invest in assets that create passive income. The idea is to build passive income so that it pays you more than your expenses and, alleviates the need for your earned income.

Now evaluate and prioritize each of the goals you identified above. In doing so, take into account:

- Its level of importance on a scale of 1 to 10 (with 1 being the most important)
- The time frame in which you want to accomplish each goal
- Current resources (money) available to support each goal
- Additional resources (money) needed to support each goal

Take time to fully answer these questions. Your answers will give you a clear understanding of how you must commit to spending your money each month. They'll force you to think it through. They'll also help you in the next step, which is to determine how much you must invest each month in order to reach your financial goals. We do this with a Goal Achievement Plan.

GUERRILLA INTELLIGENCE

Initially, when most beginners think about acquiring wealth, they look only to themselves and question whether they have what it takes to get what they want. We call this the Lone Ranger Syndrome. The answers they find are often discouraging and typically stop beginners dead in their tracks.

GUERRILLA INTELLIGENCE (cont'd)

In acquiring wealth, NO ONE DOES IT ALONE; there are no Lone Rangers. Wealthy people don't go it alone. In fact, whenever possible - which is most of the time - they use other people's money, time and creativity. They know where to go to get money. A major part of this process is learning where and how you can get the resources that will make you wealthy.

GOAL ACHIEVEMENT INVESTMENT PLAN

To forecast how much you must invest each month to reach your financial goals, list each of your specific goals:

Example 1: I will put my daughter through college. I will fully cover her tuition and books, as well as provide a monthly stipend for her living expenses such as rent, clothing, food, auto and insurance.

Example 2: I will contribute $150,000 to child literacy programs in the U.S.

Example 3: I will sponsor a race car to compete in the Indianapolis 500.

Your Financial Freedom Day

Let's take Example 1 and follow it through. Determine how much time it will take to reach each goal.

Example 1: 15 years.

The estimated cost of reaching each goal.
Example 1: A minimum of $150,000.

The rate of return you realistically expect on your investment. Refer to the chart 4-1, which follows.

Example 1: Six percent.

Chart 4-1 on the next page is a basic amortization chart that will give you a rough idea of the returns available on your investments.

Your Financial Freedom Day

Chart 4-1

Years	6%	8%	10%
18	.0026	.0021	.0016
17	.0028	.0023	.0019
16	.0031	.0026	.0021
15	.0034	.0029	.0024
14	.0038	.0032	.0027
13	.0042	.0036	.0031
12	.0047	.0041	.0036
11	.0053	.0047	.0041
10	.0060	.0054	.0048
9	.0069	.0063	.0057
8	.0080	.0074	.0067
7	.0095	.0088	.0081
6	.0114	.0107	.0100
5	.0141	.0133	.0126
4	.0181	.0173	.0166
3	.0247	.0239	.0232
2	.0377	.0369	.0361
1	.0746	.0739	.0732

* Rates of return as indicate on the chart on the previous page are for illustration purposes only. This example is not intended to represent the past or future returns of any specific investment or investment strategy.

Your Financial Freedom Day

This is the estimated cost of reaching each goal by the rate of return you realistically expect on your investment. The answer will give you a rough estimate of how much you must invest monthly to reach your financial goals.

Example: $150,000 times .0034 (6 percent rate of return for 15 years) = $510 per month that you must invest.

In summary: In order to achieve my goal of having $150,000 available in 15 years to put my daughter through college, I'll need to invest $510 each month into my daughter's college fund at a minimum 6 percent return.

Now, do the same exercise for each of your financial goals. Calculate each on a separate sheet of paper. Be sure to clearly identify the specific goal that you're estimating and keep a copy with your financial planning records.

Goal #1 - Monthly Investment Amount - Criteria

Goal #2 - Monthly Investment Amount - Criteria

Goal #3 - Monthly Investment Amount - Criteria

This type of forecasting will help you to see that you have many money-making choices. It'll also help you start making different choices for creating wealth. We'll discuss forecasting in detail later in this chapter.

By completing a goal achievement investment plan for each of your financial goals, you've taken a major step toward achieving financial freedom. In fact, you have done about half of the initial work that we require from our clients before we begin our coaching sessions. The answers you found will be the launching pad for the cycles of wealth you'll build, and will become invaluable weapons in your financial arsenal.

YOUR WEALTH ACCOUNT

You've just spent a considerable amount of time detailing your financial goals. Before we continue, there's one action everyone must take to ensure the achievement of those goals. This step is to open your first wealth account.

A wealth account is an account that you put money into to build assets. The sole purpose of a wealth account is to build wealth. You constantly add money to your wealth account, then invest it well. The passive income to help you achieve your Financial Freedom Day goal starts in your wealth account.

Opening your account may seem like a baby step, but the individuals we coach routinely tell us that it marked the difference between "dreaming" and "doing." Like the other steps in this book, it's essential! In fact, it's so important, we encourage you to celebrate in some way. Mark it in your calendar or journal. Make it an occasion. You're crossing another threshold to model the wealthy so you, too, can achieve wealth.

When you deposit your money in a savings account, it pays a meager amount of interest. A wealth account - which is typically a brokerage account, a trading account or a money-market account - pays a bit more.

Your Financial Freedom Day

However the real advantage of these types of wealth accounts is that you can easily purchase investments, often with a simple transfer. In selecting a wealth account, place a higher premium on the ease with which you can invest rather than on the interest it will bear. Today, you can find these kinds of accounts through online brokerage firms.

Here's how a wealth account works: you pay a minimum amount into your account each week, month, or whatever period you determine. Usually, monthly payments are easiest. Start right away and deposit regularly! Don't wait to open your wealth account until you've accumulated a lot of cash or have identified a particular investment. Those are excuses that hold you back and can keep you from paying yourself, building the account and amassing what you need to invest.

As it grows, you'll find yourself becoming more aware of investment and potential investment opportunities. More importantly, you'll change the way you think and put yourself in a position to quickly and aggressively invest.The only reason you take money out of a wealth account is to invest. It's not a savings account! Your wealth account is exclusively for investing and exists solely to make money for you.

We encourage parents to establish a wealth account for each of their children when that child is born. They should also teach their children, at early ages, to put a portion of their allowances or gifts, and later, earnings from part-time jobs, into their wealth accounts.

PAY YOURSELF FIRST

Now that you've opened your first wealth account, what are you going to do with it? You're going to start playing the money game by following one of our most essential money rules - Pay Yourself First.

You pay into your wealth account first, before you pay your bills, creditors or anything else. Consider it the equivalent of your mortgage, child support or any other obligation that you're required to pay. We don't care if you pay only $20 or $30 each month; set up a wealth account and pay yourself first.

Make your wealth account a priority. Even in the tightest months, pay yourself (your wealth account) first. Do it religiously! Even if you're in debt, deposit a portion of your earnings into your wealth account NOW. Remember, the amount you pay each period doesn't matter. The important factor is to form the habit of regularly depositing money into your wealth account and building up funds to invest in your future.

Can you imagine how much you would be worth if, from an early age, you'd been conditioned to pay yourself first by depositing a portion of your earnings in a wealth account?

Paying yourself first isn't just about accumulating funds to invest, although it certainly doesn't hurt. Equally important is developing the habit of taking a portion of your income and depositing it into an account that will grow your wealth. An additional benefit of paying yourself first is that it sharpens your thinking and adjusts your focus: it changes your mindset so that you start to see everything in terms of acquiring wealth, and it perfects the discipline for you to achieve it.

Experts recommend that you set aside ten percent of your income, and we agree. However, few people actually do. The citizens of Italy are a rare exception because, on the average, they save 22 percent of their earnings. Interestingly, Italy is one of the few countries that operates in the black because they don't rely on fixed income, pensions or retirement plans.

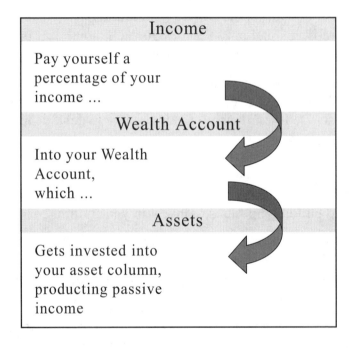

Income

Pay yourself a percentage of your income ...

Wealth Account

Into your Wealth Account, which ...

Assets

Gets invested into your asset column, producting passive income

The chart above illustrates how paying yourself first works. When you receive income, you pay a percentage of it to yourself in your wealth account. You may hold the money in your wealth account so it can draw interest until you find good investments. When the timing is right, you invest the money in your wealth account to produce passive income.

Let us repeat that a wealth account should be independent of your checking or savings accounts. We highly recommend brokerage accounts or money-market accounts that allow your assets to be quickly used for investments.

GUERRILLA TACTIC

If you're the parent of young children, break the cycle of financial illiteracy by teaching your kids to start and maintain wealth accounts. Since the educational systems for young children don't offer financial literacy programs, the burden of developing their financial knowledge is on you.

Start by getting your kids to form the habit of putting a percentage of all money they receive in wealth accounts. Even if they only get allowances, have them deposit 50 percent each week. Motivate them and reinforce their new habit by periodically showing them how much their wealth account has grown.

If you don't teach your kids, who will? Think of it as part of your parental duties and your inheritance. Showing them how to form life-long patterns will enable them to live prosperously. This, along with positive financial information, will secure their future unlike any other type of education can. See www.moneycampforkids.com.

Your Financial Freedom Day

**"As adults, our conditioning is so ingrained . . .
if we want to adopt something new,
we've got to change our mind.
Kids are in a great position because they're just
making up their mind."**

Bob Proctor

HELPFUL TIP

Instruct your financial institution to transfer money from your main account to your wealth account via an automatic debit system. With automatic transfers, you don't have to worry about forgetting to make deposits into your wealth account. Plus, you won't have to go the trouble of writing out deposit slips or mailing or physically making deposits.

Set up all your accounts online so you can review them at any time and at your convenience. It's fun to review your finances while you're in your pajamas. With online banking, you can also make account-to-account transfers if you decide to place additional funds in your wealth account. Most financial institutions offer online banking at no additional charge.

YOUR COMMITMENT

To build the foundation for a lifetime of wealth, commit to paying yourself first. Do it in writing. Make it tangible by filling in and signing a formal commitment to yourself. By doing so, you'll have physical evidence you can look at and touch that affirms your new commitment. This is more powerful than simply having an idea, a memory or good intentions.

Copy the following form, or make a similar form of your choosing, and insert:

- ➢ Your name
- ➢ The institution where you opened your wealth account
- ➢ How much you will contribute each week or month
- ➢ Sign and date it

Place your commitment where you can see it easily and each time you see it, imagine how rich and happy you're going to be.

By _____

I will open up my first wealth account with

_____ (company)

and will invest $_____ /month.

To be even more proactive, I will set up this wealth account as an "auto debit" to ensure that it happens.

_____   _____
Signature   Date

FINANCIAL FORECASTING

Now you have your vision, have set your goals, opened your first wealth account and know that you must pay yourself first. Next, it's time to purposefully design and forecast how you're going to do what you need to do with what you currently have.

Forecasting is a guerrilla tactic. It's an entirely different concept than budgeting, even though you're still working with numbers. In the old Industrial Age model of budgeting, most people looked at what they had in hand from their paychecks, then looked at their current obligations to see how far they could stretch the money. Putting some savings aside was about as sophisticated and forward-looking as budgeting allowed. Often the result was a smaller vision and shrinking expectations. Making do. Settling for.

Forecasting, on the other hand, pushes you into the future that you want and shows you precisely what's needed to get there. You'll soon see how that's the driver behind your wealth-building plan. And a paycheck just won't be enough to cut it.

Using your financial baseline - whether it's good, bad or ugly - forecast your current spending habits. Chart exactly how much you're spending and include what you're spending it on. How much do you spend on your housing, the place where you work, your kids' education, your clothing, education and debts? Discover where your money is going. Be prepared to be shocked.

Your Financial Freedom Day

Write everything down. Then put it in an Excel document, print it out from your accounting system or hand write it on a piece of paper. This is your baseline. This is what you currently do right now. It's safe for you to be brutally honest and real because it's about to get much better!

Spending Category	Current
Pay Yourself First	$0.00
Tithing	$0.00
Emergency Fund	$0.00
College Fund	$0.00
Tax	$3,056.00
Rent	$1,500.00
Daycare	$860.00
Car Payment #1	$371.40
Car Payment #2	$144.29
Utilities	$85.00
Cable	$65.00
Cell Phone	$89.00
Credit Card #1	$200.00
Credit Card #2	$200.00
Loan	$350.00
Healthcare	$274.00
Food	$500.00
Gas	$300.00
Entertainment	$200.00
Total Expense	$8,194.69
Total Income	$9,550.00
Difference	$1,355.31

Your Financial Freedom Day

Now that you have your current spending habits spelled out in front of you, we're going to re-build them to work toward achieving your goals. We're going to purposefully forecast your spending and use every single penny that you have to its full advantage.

We'll assume the example represents your spending. Our first thought as mentors and coaches is, where did that "extra" $1,355.31 go? Did you spend it? Is it in a savings account? How is this accounted for?

Our second thought is, why are you paying so much in taxes? If you're running a home business, why don't you use a business bank account and write off those legal expenses? We'll go more into that in future chapters.

Our third thought is, you didn't pay yourself first, nor did you contribute anything toward your recently established goals.

Let's start by detailing where you MUST spend your money and how much you MUST spend in each instance. This list will consist of those essential items that you must have to live. Next, examine where you're overspending. Focus on your old spending habits that no longer make sense and see how much money you'll free up if you STOP spending in this manner.

Once you know where you are - the unvarnished truth about it - you can reallocate your money to get you where you want to go. We're going to purposefully spend the money that you just rescued from the depths of poor spending by putting it into the wealth account that you established previously in this chapter. Welcome to the world of conscious spending!

Spending Category	Current	Forecasted	
Pay Yourself	$0.00	$2,725.00	Into a Wealth First Account designated for assets
Tithing	$0.00	$955.00	10 percent
Emergency	$0.00	$200.00	Until you have 3 months of income into this fund
College Fund	$0.00	$510.00	Per goal setting forecast
Tax	$3,056.00	$1,146.00	Took advantage of tax strategies to decrease
Rent	$1,500.00	$1,500.00	
Daycare	$860.00	$860.00	
Car Payment #1	$371.40	$0.00	
Car Payment #2	$144.29	$0.00	
Utilities	$85.00	$60.00	
Cable	$65.00	$35.00	
Cell Phone	$89.00	$59.00	
Credit Card #1	$200.00	$0.00	
Credit Card #2	$200.00	$0.00	
Loan	$350.00	$675.00	Re-financed all debts into one loan
Healthcare	$274.00	$0.00	Joined spouse's healthcare program
Food	$500.00	$425.00	Joined Costco & bought in bulk
Gas	$300.00	$300.00	
Entertainment	$200.00	$100.00	
Total Expense	$8,194.69	$9,550.00	
Total Income	$9,550.00	$9,550.00	
Difference	$1,355.31	$0.00	

Your Financial Freedom Day

As you can see from the example above, we made many changes in how and where the money was being allocated. We intentionally spent in every category and used every penny that was earned in a productive way. While these are only examples of the ways in which you can decrease expenses and re-allocate money to your wealth accounts, we think that it powerfully illustrates the point of how important it is to implement this step. In strategizing for just five minutes, we found $4,390 to allocate to essential spending categories.

When you truly forecast, you'll want all of your money to be allocated to a spending category. Your difference should be ZERO. By purposefully spending every penny, you eliminate all emotional spending. In the example, we took all the remaining income and placed it in the Pay Yourself First category, which will allow your assets to increase at an accelerated rate.

After you complete the exercises, state your observations.

1.   How did it feel to make decisions about your spending?

_____

2.   What surprised you?

_____

_____

3.   Did you procrastinate?

_____

Your Financial Freedom Day

4.   What made you hesitate?

_____

_____

5.   What were you unwilling to decide and why?

_____

_____

6.   What will you do differently?

_____

_____

Advanced forecasting includes breaking out your income and expenses into personal vs. business categories, and for some of you, multiple businesses. Advanced forecasting is driven by maximizing your tax strategies to take advantage of every possible business deduction, instead of paying for business expenses out of your personal accounts.

The following page will give you an example of what that might look like.

		Trust		
	Personal	**ABC S-Corp**	**223 LLC**	**Total**
Income				
Rental Income				
Happy Ave.			$ 500.	$ 500.
Glad Blvd.			$ 750.	$ 750.
Excited Crt.			$ 800.	$ 800.
John's Net	$2,500.			$ 2,500.
Joan's Net	$2,700.			$ 2,700.
Business Revenue		$2,800.		$ 2,800
Gross Income	**$5,200.**	**$2,800.**	**$2,050.**	**$10,050.**
Expenses				
Home Mortgage	$ 600.			$ 600.
Home Office	$ 125.			$ 125.
Home Assoc. Fees			$ 800.	$ 800.
LLC Mortgage (PITI)		$ 150.		$ 150.
Utilities	$ 57.			$ 57.
Water	$ 36.			$ 36.
Sewage	$ 48.			$ 48.
Electricity	$ 25.			$ 25.
Auto Expenses LLC Car			$ 468.	$ 468.
Joan's Car	$ 67.		$ 98.	$ 165.
LLCs Ins.		$450.		$ 450.
Joan's Ins.	$ 50.			$ 50.
Plates		$ 58.	$ 82.	$ 140.
Gas	$ 6.		$ 28.	$ 34.
Parking	$ 50.			$ 50.
Education		$ 49.		$ 49.
Totals	**$1,064.**	**$707.**	**$1,476.**	**$3,247.**

Your Financial Freedom Day

As you can see, forecasting is a strategic and ongoing process that will change as you and your financial results grow. Without forecasting, you'll continue to overpay in taxes, overspend emotionally and squander more of your money. In our opinion, forecasting is one of the most strategic steps in creating guerrilla wealth.

In our experience, this is where the majority of our clients need the most support, and once they've mastered it, find it the easiest to maintain. Please don't hesitate to ask for help with this step. Visit www.liveoutloud.com, send an email to info@liveoutloud.com or call 1-888-262-2402 to see what tools you may need to help you in this area.

SHARE YOUR VISION AND FORECAST YOUR WEALTH

In the chart on the previous page, you get a glimpse of the kind of high-end tactics you'll learn about as you advance in your wealth building. Don't be alarmed if it seems foreign to you. We simply want to start conditioning you for your own future wealth.

Now that you've developed some understanding of forecasting, let's repeat the exercise we completed at the beginning of this chapter. State your financial vision. In the space provided, explain your financial vision using clear and concise language. For example, "I want an income of $20,000 a month, three homes and my kids to be set for life," or, "I want to leave nothing behind." Whatever your vision is for your financial future, write it down.

Write your vision below. Then share your vision with three to five people who want a similar life.

_____

_____

_____

_____

_____

_____

_____

_____

_____

_____

_____

_____

REVISIT YOUR GOALS

Let's also return to the exercise you completed in the beginning of this chapter, Your Financial Gap. In that exercise, you were asked to determine your Financial Freedom Day. Now that you've nearly completed this chapter, complete that exercise again. See how your answers differ, and when you're finished, complete and sign a declaration, a commitment to your financial independence. The questions again are:

Your Financial Freedom Day

1.   How much money (cash flow) do you want to
        receive each month? _____

2.   What do you want your
        net worth to be?   _____

3.   By what age?   _____

4.   By what day,
        month and year?   _____

Now declare your Financial Freedom Day. Create this form on your computer, print it out and fill it in. Post it prominently where you can easily see it. Carry a copy with you. Tape it to your refrigerator and to the dashboard of your car. Review it each morning when you get up, at every meal and before you go to bed. Always have the message in the forefront of your mind.

Certificate

I, _____

do hereby decree that on

_____ of the year _____ ,

I will be financially free.

This means that I will have

a passive income of

$ _____ per month

and a net worth of $ _____

_____   _____

Signature   Date

SUCCESS STORIES

Socorro Curiel

"I was slaving away day and night as a full-time engineer in Silicon Valley. After I learned about the concept of a Financial Freedom Day, the first thing I did was to set a date to leave my job. However, before that date could become a reality, I had to figure out how much money I'd need to leave by my target date.

With my Financial Freedom Day set, I got aggressive. To create cash flow, I picked up rental properties and by staying at my job, I easily qualified for mortgages. By working with a mortgage broker, I found that I could qualify for up to six loans. If I moved quickly, I calculated, the cash flow from six properties would bring in enough for me to leave my job.

When I hit my cash-flow target of $2,000 per month, I left my job as planned. Since then, I've set a new Financial Freedom Day in 2006, when I plan to make $10,000 per month in rental income. I have no doubt that I will reach that goal. I have my wealth team in place and I'm on track to be a millionaire by December of 2004. Since March of 2002, I have created four companies with 15 rental properties. I've done it by partnering with others, including my sister for the first property. In the meantime, I've picked up two more partners and created two more companies.

To achieve my first financial freedom day, the biggest shift I had to make was to stop thinking of myself as an hourly person. I had to see my life as a business, and look earnestly for opportunities to invest in properties that would give me both equity and cash flow. I had to tell people that 'I am a real estate investor,' which initially felt strange, but soon started to make things happen."

Shawn Studer

"In December of 2002, I first formulated my plan. It was right after I joined one of Loral's first Big Tables and realized that I would have to change if I wanted to create enough income to retire from my job as an airline flight attendant. My first move was to shift my focus. Instead of socking away money by taking every flight assignment I could, I began giving many of my trips away and started looking for property instead.

I projected how many rental properties I would need and then got very clear on what I wanted and needed. When I put all my ideas on paper, I was astonished to find that they all could be achieved. Once I knew that I could do it, it didn't take long to find my niche and the moment I got clear, things started happening.

After 23 years as a flight attendant, I retired in July of 2004. I now have 35 properties, and am starting to build houses. I've doubled my net worth, and am slowly increasing my passive income. After starting with no passive income, I'm now at around $4,000 per month and I've set a target to quickly double that amount.

The key for me was making the projections. I wasn't clear and used the projections to define what I wanted and how I would accomplish it. I specifically asked, 'How much income will it take for me to retire,' and I calculated how many houses that would equal. The shift in my focus from the number of flights to the number of houses was key. I changed my thinking from 'making money' to 'creating wealth' and it enabled me to get the results I sought."

SUMMING UP

Your Financial Freedom Day is the time you've always dreamed of, when you get to lead the "want to" life and not be forced to live the life you "have to" live. Start by identifying your vision and setting your goals. When you know exactly where you're headed, it's easier to find the quickest and most direct road to get what you seek. It'll also help you to identify potential obstacles in your path so that you can avoid them or reduce their impact.

Clearly state your Financial Freedom Day goals. Determine how much you must invest each month to reach your financial goals. Pay yourself first. Develop the habit of taking a portion of your income and depositing it into a wealth account, which is separate from your checking or saving accounts. Your wealth account is the place where you hold money that you can invest to produce passive income.

Your Financial Forecasting assures that you're keeping more of your money to invest in assets by taking advantage of better tax strategies, lowering your personal expenses and reducing your emotional spending.

Your Financial Freedom Day

LORAL'S LEARNING LOOP

What are three things you learned from this chapter?

_____

_____

_____

_____

_____

What three actions will you take as a result of this chapter?

_____

_____

_____

_____

_____

List the dates when you will begin and complete your three actions.

_____

_____

_____

To whom will you be accountable?

_____

5

Managing Your Lifestyle Cycle

*"Build your assets
and then build your lifestyle."*

This chapter may be a surprise for you!

We're going to talk about another primary principle of the wealthy, and the skills that go with it, but it's counter-intuitive to how most of America lives. The principle is managing your LifeStyle Cycle.

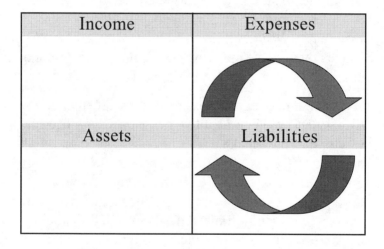

Income	Expenses
Assets	Liabilities

A LifeStyle Cycle is a remnant of the Industrial Age model of financial success. Here's how it works: you earn money to buy bigger houses, fancy cars and more stuff, which increases your liabilities, which increases your monthly expenses. As you can see from the diagram above, this perpetuates a cycle of earning, spending, earning, spending.

A LifeStyle Cycle increases your standard of living,

not your bank account. In a LifeStyle Cycle, your liabilities, rather than your assets, are the forces that drive your financial machine. Those debts can be the single greatest factor in preventing you from acquiring wealth. With bad debt (consumer debt) siphoning off the money each month, you can't build the assets you need to create wealth.

Most people never break their LifeStyle Cycle. In fact, most people would rather live in the right neighborhood, look good and have all the right trimmings to stay in a LifeStyle Cycle. They'd never consider stopping for a moment in order to create a sustainable Wealth Cycle. And they have no idea what it costs them in the long run – not just what they spend, but what they lose by not building wealth first.

Over and over, we've seen clients get stuck in the LifeStyle Cycle in one of two primary ways. The first way is that they make a lot of money and spend it all on their lifestyles. They don't go into debt, but they don't create assets. We saw this scenario repeatedly during the dot.com era when high-income earners were overspending on million-dollar homes and the hottest cars. However, when the dot.com turned into the dot bomb, they lost everything. They crashed because they had not built on a solid foundation.

The second way that we've seen the impact of the LifeStyle Cycle is in the accumulation of excessive consumer debt. In this cycle, individuals don't earn enough to cover their spending. So they support their lifestyle choices by charging their purchases to credit cards. Some actually come to regard their credit lines

Managing Your Lifestyle Cycle

as some sort of "income" that's available on demand. You can hear these people say things like, "Oh, I can buy that. I have the money," when in fact what they have is a bit of credit available on one or more of their cards.

As we alluded to above, in our consumer-based economy, most people get lost. They get the concepts of wealth building backwards and do the opposite of what they should do to grow rich. When they start to acquire money, they also begin to pile up debt. "We've finally made it," they seem to shout and then they promptly reward themselves for their long, hard struggles. With credit cards firmly in hand, they go shopping, determined to buy even bigger homes, more luxurious cars, exotic vacations, the latest electronics and all those other cool toys that come with affluence. It's like a passion or a mission that must immediately be fulfilled.

It's the 21st century version of "What will the neighbors think?" or "Keeping up with the Joneses *and* the Smiths *and* their entire social set." It's all about appearances.

After they charge their hearts out, the bills roll in. They try to pay for all their new stuff from limited income, which usually doesn't work. In most cases, there's simply insufficient income to cover all of their debt. And with compound interest working *against* them instead of *for* them, soon the debt is completely unmanageable.

Even worse, this house-of-cards living requires very little – a medical emergency, or an unexpected repair on the house – to topple an unsustainable lifestyle. A major problem, such as the layoff of a spouse, can bring it all down. This kind of lifestyle may look carefree, but it comes with a heavy cost: stress, marital problems, divorce, loss of self-respect and a variety of other problems.

You may already know personally that consumer debt is a trap. If consumer debt is your problem, I have good news for you. You can turn your financial life around! So if you've ever despaired of keeping up, not with the Joneses, but with your creditors, this chapter is for you.

We're going to give you an unflinching view of life as a debtor and what you can do about it. This may be a difficult subject for you, but guerrilla wealth is honest wealth that will sustain you, not the thin veneer of a "designer life." Honestly, which would you really prefer to have?

If you're addicted to credit card spending, even if it seems to be in control, you must come to terms with the reality that this kind of debt is bad debt. It doesn't generate income. Debt robs you of the resources that could be building wealth. It also steals time by delaying your ability to start building wealth.

Take a deep breath. Your wealth vision is possible, even if you seem to be drowning in debt right now. In this chapter, we're going to show you how to break your LifeStyle Cycle and eliminate your bad debt.

Managing Your Lifestyle Cycle

DEBT

Before we continue any further, let's stop, step back and refresh your memory about a critical concept that we previously introduced: good and bad debt. For this part of your guerrilla wealth training, it's absolutely imperative that you understand the difference between good and bad debt.

Good debt is debt acquired through the purchase of assets that you invest to produce passive income (income made through your money and investments). Examples of good debt are mortgages on dwellings that you lease to generate rental income and lines of credit that you obtain to strategically enhance your business growth – for instance, to buy inventory, equipment, or competing or complementary businesses.

WARNING: If you're an investor who's incurring good debt, be aware that you may reach a point in your growth where the amount of debt you take on (your debt-to-income ratios) can make it difficult for you to obtain additional financing. This frequently occurs with real estate investors who purchase a number of properties too quickly and find that lenders consider the amounts they owe to be excessive. We'll discuss debt ratios and leveraging debt in Chapter 6, Building A Wealth Cycle Foundation.

Bad debt is typically consumer debt and similar obligations that do not produce revenue. It arises when you buy items now, mostly consumables for your lifestyle, but pay for them later. The most apparent examples of bad debt occur when you charge your retail therapy, vacation, entertainment and restaurant flings. These expenditures may give you a lift, make you feel glamorous or impress others, but they don't increase your wealth.

Bad debt generally carries high interest rates and offers deceptively alluring low-payment amounts that can run forever and a day. When you pay the minimum requested, you're mainly paying interest and barely reducing what you owe. We've even seen some cases where the minimum payment on a credit card is *less* than the interest, which means the debt gets larger, even without additional purchases!

According to estimates, 80 percent of Americans are in severe consumer debt. Savings are minimal, billions in consumer debt are owed, and only a relatively small percentage of the populace is actively trying to reverse it. We invite you to join that minority.

GUERRILLA INTELLIGENCE

Look at bad debt as if you've gained 40 pounds over the last few years. As a result, you're overweight, and if you want to look smashing for the upcoming reunion, you'll have to make some changes. You'll have to cut back on calories, adjust your diet and spend more time in the gym. You must get busy, because the reunion is approaching. If you continue what you've been doing, you'll never lose weight.

GUERRILLA INTELLIGENCE (cont'd)

Similarly, if you're drowning in debt, have $70,000 in liabilities and want to build wealth, you must make lifestyle changes. You must change your lifestyle habits of over-consumption, tone up your finances and get your Wealth Cycle in shape. You need to make lifestyle changes and start putting money away instead of always paying it out. Bottom line: both are a result of over-consumptive behaviors.

THE SYMPTOMS

When you hear yourself saying any of the following, think bad debt:

> ➢ "How did I get here? I had more money when I was making $20,000 a year."
> ➢ "I can't seem to hold onto money."
> ➢ "I'll invest when I have a bunch of cash."
> ➢ "The money comes in; the money flies out."
> ➢ "A windfall is going to get me out of this debt problem."

Managing Your Lifestyle Cycle

When you catch yourself doing any of the following, think bad debt:

> ➤ Cycling your credit cards (credit card roulette).
> ➤ Refinancing your home on a regular basis.
> ➤ Repeatedly consolidating your debts.
> ➤ Declaring bankruptcy.
> ➤ Never projecting where you want to be or forecasting your financial future. You don't even think about it.

Ask yourself the following questions and write your answers below:

1. What is your LifeStyle Cycle conversation about money?

2. When you focus on what you want, do you find you can't afford it?

3. Do you always have excuses to try to explain why you're not moving forward? If so, what are they?

_____

_____

_____

What psychological conditioning has led to your LifeStyle Cycle behaviors? Examples could be:

> ➤ My father went bankrupt.
> ➤ My uncle always borrows money and never pays it back.
> ➤ My single mother had to work three jobs.
> ➤ My parents couldn't afford to pay my college tuition.
> ➤ We couldn't afford to go on summer vacations.

Let's also explore the reason for your problems. In the space below, list the habits that have been keeping you addicted to your financially destructive LifeStyle Cycle. Be completely and totally honest in this exercise or you'll lose the potential benefit of finally facing up to your personal financial reality.

Examples might be:

1. I use credit cards consistently to purchase goods and services that I want, but can't afford. If this is the case, exercise more self-control, and if that isn't realistic, consider destroying your credit cards.

2. I overspend to fulfill an emotional need, not because of a survival need. If this applies to you, something major is missing in your life and you may need to seek counseling to discover and seek a cure for your problem.

Now, write below what conditioning of yours has shaped your LifeStyle Cycle.

_____

_____

_____

_____

_____

_____

_____

_____

What will you do to change it?

_____

_____

_____

If, after completing the above exercises, you feel trapped by consumer debt, a number of options are available to help you eliminate that debt. While each of the following options is a viable way to eliminate your debt, please be careful because they can actually turn against you when abused and could keep you in debt indefinitely. Examine these alternatives closely and carefully, and only use those that strategically fit into your plan.

CONSUMER DEBT OPTIONS

Credit Card Roulette

When people owe money on a credit card that carries a high interest rate (let's say 20 percent) and transfer the amount they owe to another card with a lower rate (10 percent), we call it credit card roulette. Like their cousins in Las Vegas, many are desperate or love to live life on the edge. They may fully intend to pay the debts they've rolled over, but that's generally not what occurs.

Transferring debt to get a lower interest rate is not a bad idea if you control your lifestyle and don't take on added debt, but we all know how elusive discipline can be. In our experience, after making balance transfers, cardholders usually lose no time in running up their original high-interest cards again. At first, the lower rate and reduced monthly payments provide temporary relief, but when the additional debt from the initial cards kick in, the hole of debt suddenly becomes a money pit. Over time, a history of cycling credit cards can catch up with you because lenders who notice the pattern may no longer extend you credit.

Unfortunately, in playing credit card roulette, most cardholders only address the results of the problem, not its cause. They continue their lavish lifestyles and don't stop spending more than they earn. Since they can't pay their debt, they can't pay themselves first, which is essential if they want to build wealth.

Refinancing Your Home

Refinancing your home is an excellent way of consolidating debt. However, too many people don't control their borrowing after they refinance. When they clear their debt, they begin spending again and incurring more credit card debt. As they keep spending, their debt spirals until they have to refinance again – and again.

The cycle of refinancing has inherent problems. First, at some point, serial refinancers use up all the equity they built and can no longer get additional credit. Or if they get credit, they're charged exorbitant interest rates, which cause their debt to further soar. They could be forced to sell their homes, and forced sales attract vultures who are experts at preying on and fleecing the financially distressed.

Since home equity often makes up all or part of many homeowners' nest eggs, frequent refinancers may find themselves with less money when they most need it, when their moneymaking years are behind them. In effect, they may pay for their computers or consumer goodies some 30 years later, when those items are long gone . . . but not financially forgotten.

Managing Your Lifestyle Cycle

Consolidating Your Debt

Companies known as debt consolidators will take all of your debt and collapse it so you only have to make a single, comfortable monthly payment. Then they go to your creditors, negotiate to reduce outstanding debt and pay it off. In turn, you pay the consolidators each month until your entire debt is clear.

Again, people tend to acquire additional debt after consolidation so the old debt cycle resurfaces once more. Frequently, another downside of debt consolidation is that you end up paying less principal and more interest so it takes forever to wipe your slate clean. This phenomenon occurs because after consolidation you make lower monthly payments than before you consolidated your debt.

GUERRILLA INTELLIGENCE

Generally speaking, people can be divided into two camps: those who **PAY** interest or those who **GET PAID** interest. To become wealthy, the goal is to be paid interest, to be on the receiving end.

When you collect interest, you're adding to your assets and increasing your wealth. You become the bank, and you know that banks are in the business of making money. If you pay interest, it depletes your resources.

The purpose of this book is to help you become someone who gets paid interest, and the best place to start is by eliminating your bad debt.

Managing Your Lifestyle Cycle

Bankruptcy

When the subject of debt is discussed, many of us think of bankruptcy because today, we seem to be in the midst of a bankruptcy epidemic – an epidemic that's continually growing and shows no signs of easing.

Bankruptcy is not a debt solution. In fact, it shouldn't be considered as an option until you have fully explored every other possible option. Declaring bankruptcy can seriously disrupt your life and ruin your credit. Although you can recover, it may take years. Generally, it takes seven years until you can rebuild the type of credit that can accelerate your creation of wealth.

Bankruptcy has more subtle, but equally harmful, implications. Many people are personally offended by bankruptcy and it influences their opinions on everything from doing business with you to giving you a job. Bankruptcy also doesn't free you from all debt – most importantly taxes, which carry substantial penalties and interest. Furthermore, large special interests are constantly lobbying Congress for bankruptcy "reform," so by the time you decide to file, the protection granted could significantly change.

The most commonly known types of bankruptcy are Chapter 7 and Chapter 13. Chapter 7 is personal financial dissolution, and is also known as liquidation bankruptcy. Chapter 13 bankruptcy is personal financial reorganization, and is also known as wage-earner bankruptcy.

The other thing that you should consider before ever declaring any type of bankruptcy is to note where you'll be 6 months, 12 months and three years from now. Here's a quick story to illustrate this point: a client of ours came to us with a very discouraging situation. When she was 23 years old, she found herself a single mom with a four-month-old child. To make matters worse, within the next six weeks she was also out of a job because her company went out of business.

When she took a look at her finances, she came to the conclusion that she would not be able to make it. She made the choice to declare bankruptcy. The total that she owed was a mere $15,000, but in her current situation and mindset she could see no other option.

Within six months, she secured a very lucrative career, and within two years, she married. She was more than able to get herself out of debt at that time, yet it was too late. Had she simply had the capacity to find a short-term solution to her immediate needs, she could have avoided the hassle, embarrassment and long-term, negative effects of a bankruptcy.

Even with her current income levels and our creative financial strategies, this ding on her credit excludes her from many lucrative opportunities. It will be at least another five years before she can take full advantage of the use of her credit.

IMPORTANT: If you're contemplating bankruptcy, please fully consider all other options of debt elimination first and *consult with a lawyer who specializes in bankruptcy.* Make sure you know the facts before you consider filing for bankruptcy, because you may have to live with the consequences for years.

Managing Your Lifestyle Cycle

CREDIT REPAIR

Many people who are deeply in debt need credit repair. Credit repair companies can help you fix your bad credit. Many legitimate organizations run great programs that will do exactly what they promise, which is to get your credit fixed.

Unfortunately, dealing with credit repair companies can be risky. While many ethical, credible agencies really help, just as many are shady and ruthless. They don't deliver what they promise and can make your credit worse. Many charge high fees upfront, which can cost you thousands of dollars, and then do little or nothing to fix your credit.

GUERRILLA TACTIC

Before you sign on with any credit repairer, get solid references from people you know and trust. Don't just go with the first company you find. Comparison shop. The difference in the cost to you can be substantial. Don't base your decision solely on price. Look first for a firm that will deliver and actually repair your credit.

Be wary of online credit repair companies that don't have brick and mortar offices. The Internet has been flooded with tons of firms that promise to repair your credit, then take your money and fail to deliver.

Managing Your Lifestyle Cycle

At Live Out Loud, we provide experienced credit repair to our coaching clients. For further information about becoming a client of Live Out Loud, contact us at info@liveoutloud.com and we'll send you the names of credit repair agents that our clients have recommended.

THE PATH OUT OF DEBT

Most people with debt problems rarely try to determine their exact financial position or where they would like to go financially. They're so caught up in their LifeStyle Cycle, or their juggling acts to keep afloat, that they can't imagine finding a positive solution that will enable them to build wealth. Many would be so grateful to end the pain and panic of debt, they don't think much further than that one issue.

If you're currently in debt, it may have never been clear to you that you can make a conscious choice now to end your role as a debtor in the economy and become a lender instead. Make the decision, then take the steps to get out of debt. By diligently employing basic debt elimination measures, you can get out of the debt cycle within three to seven years, and at the same time, start to build your Wealth Cycle.

➢ Be unemotional about eliminating your debt, especially if your feelings got you into this mess. Think of it as a pure business venture, as a matter of simply applying dollars and cents to abolish your debt.

Managing Your Lifestyle Cycle

➤ Commit to putting a debt plan in place, following it and letting it work its magic. Atrophy your debt muscles, open your mind and learn to think differently. Then together, we can start to build your Wealth Cycle muscles.

➤ Remember that while it took you just a short amount of time to rack up the debt, it will take a longer amount of time to get out of it and repair your credit.

Here's how it's done. Change from a LifeStyle Cycle to a Wealth Cycle in three simple steps:

1. Begin a debt elimination plan to get out of debt.
2. Simultaneously, build the new habit of putting money into a wealth account every month. Don't wait; start NOW to begin the process of building your first Wealth Cycle.
3. Form the habit of paying yourself first into that wealth account.

Ready, go . . . let's get rid of this debt!

GETTING OUT OF DEBT 5-STEP PLAN

If you're in debt, we strongly encourage you to follow our five-step debt elimination process. Although many processes exist, our approach allows you to live in abundance while you eliminate your bad, consumer debt.

In the previous chapter, we asked you to create your

Managing Your Lifestyle Cycle

financial baseline, organize a filing cabinet to store all your financial records, and complete a financial forecast. If you haven't done so, do so immediately. It will make our debt elimination process easier for you.

Follow the five steps below, whether or not you now have consumer debt. If you don't have consumer debt, complete these steps and then teach the process to two other people who have consumer debt. By doing so, you'll be helping to break the bad-debt stranglehold on our society. You'll also strengthen your own good habits by more thoroughly learning them and by becoming more publicly associated with this process

Step 1

In the chart on the next page, we want you to list all of your consumer debt (credit cards, loans ... as previously described.) We've given you an example and suggest you finish the exercise with your own consumer debt ... inserting one debt in each box.

The Debt Elimination Box should include:

1. The name of the creditor.
2. How much you owe.
3. Your minimum monthly payment.
4. The interest percentage rate.
5. The factoring number, which is your total amount of debt divided by the minimum monthly payment required.

GUERRILLA WEALTH

Managing Your Lifestyle Cycle

Name of Debt:	VISA
Total Amount:	$7,000.
Min. Payment:	$200.
Interest Rate:	9%
Factoring #:	35

Name of Debt	Total Amount	Min. Payment	Interest Rate	Factoring #

Managing Your Lifestyle Cycle

Step 2

Divide the "Total Amount" of the debt by the "Minimum Payment" of each bad debt. This gives you a factoring number.

$$\frac{\$7,000}{200} = 35 \text{ (Factoring Number)}$$

Do this with every debt.

Step 3

Review all of your consumer debt listed on the previous two pages. Take the debt with the lowest factoring number and that will be your first priority in payoff. In the space provided, list the debt in order of the factoring number ... with the lowest appearing in the number 1 spot and the debt with the highest factoring number in the number 8 spot.

Priority Order of Payoff	Name of Debt	Factoring Number	Min. Payment
1.			
2.			
3.			
4.			
5.			
6.			
7.			
8.			

Total Debt Payment: _____

Step 4

We encourage you allocate $200 of your current spending to accelerate (jumpstart) your debt elimination plan. This will go a long way in eliminating your debt ... really!

Step 5

With your "Priority Order of Payoff" in tact, take the debt listed in the first spot and apply the $200 we asked you to allocate in Step 4 to the minimum payment listed with this debt. For instance, if your minimum payment is $350 and you add $200, you'll be paying a $550 payment on that debt until it's paid in full ... all the while making minimum payments on each of the other bad debts you have listed.

When you're finished paying off the debt in the number one spot, take the amount you were paying on the number 1 debt and add it to the minimum payment of the debt in the number two spot and so on until you totally eliminate all of your bad debt.

You need to be very clear about the amount of money you will allocate to your debt-elimination plan. Please fill in the blanks below.

Total of Minimum Payments: $ _____

Plus $ _____200_____

Monthly Debt-Elimination
Contribution: = $ _____

Managing Your Lifestyle Cycle

Congratulations! You are now on your way out of your Lifestyle Cycle.

In the space provided, write a commitment statement to yourself about your debt elimination plan.

_____

_____

_____

_____

_____

_____

_____

Signature	Date

What do you need to shift in your thinking so that you ensure you never end up in debt from this point forward?

_____

_____

_____

_____

_____

_____

Managing Your Lifestyle Cycle

Now that I am debt-free and it is one year later,

because I have paid myself first, I now have

$ _____ **to invest.**

GO CREATE MORE

As you begin your five-step plan and commit monthly toward eliminating your debt, we'd like you to start thinking out of the box and ask yourself, "What else can I do to create more income while managing my LifeStyle Cycle?" Focus on creating, growing and building wealth, rather than on just finding ways to pay your monthly debt.

As you do this, you'll begin to focus on the opposite of a LifeStyle Cycle, which is a Wealth Cycle. We want to teach you to build a Wealth Cycle. We call it a "Wealth Cycle" because you use your income to build assets, then reinvest those assets and create wealth. However, before you can create a Wealth Cycle, you must deal with your LifeStyle Cycle and eliminate your bad debt. We'll cover wealth foundation and acceleration cycles in detail in the next chapters.

Managing Your Lifestyle Cycle

COMMITMENT TO LIVING DEBT FREE

Write your personal statement of commitment and live faithfully by it. It's a commitment to yourself and your financial well-being.

Commit to your debt elimination plan. Promise to eliminate your debt and state the reasons why you've decided to do so. At times, you'll be tempted to use your credit cards or assume some additional debt. When they arise, remember your commitment and reread your statement to remind yourself and support your weak resolve.

Give copies of your commitment statement to your closest friends or advisors to whom you will be financially accountable. Give them permission to question you about your debt and speak honestly with them. Think of them as your controls, helpers who will keep you in line. Now write your commitment statement below. State precisely what you will do to eliminate your bad debt and never get into bad debt again.

_____

_____

_____

_____

_____

_____

_____   _____

Signature   Date

Managing Your Lifestyle Cycle

Now examine how you need to change your thinking so that you never end up in this kind of debt again.

Describe those changes below.

1. How do you plan to make the necessary changes?

   _____

   _____

   _____

   _____

2. What results do you expect those changes to bring?

   _____

   _____

   _____

   _____

3. Describe the steps you'll take to make sure that you stick with your plan.

   _____

   _____

   _____

   _____

SUCCESS STORY

Shawn Moore

"When I got divorced, I was a middle-aged woman. Since my life had been turned upside-down, I started taking a lot of personal growth training, which I paid for with credit cards. I ended up with a lot of debt. When Loral and I reviewed my debt, she took it all in stride. She showed me that much of my debt was business-related, which I'd never considered. 'You are in business, so act like it,' Loral explained. This revelation changed everything for me!

I learned how to separate my business from my personal debt. Seeing my debt as a business expense helped me to realize that debt is a necessary part of starting a new business. It taught me that my life is a business and the expenses I incur are investments in my education and development. Then, Loral took me through her very simple debt-reduction method and we created a plan. We decided how to communicate with my creditors and negotiate lower interest rates, and discussed the options for restructuring my debt. Within minutes, I emerged from what felt like a bottomless pit with new hope and I began living my life as a businessperson.

When I started reducing my debt, I stopped constantly thinking about it. This gave me the energy to create a successful wealth creation plan. I now understand that I must be in control of my debt and have a plan for building wealth. That's a completely different attitude for me and it's greatly improved my life!"

SUMMING UP

The money you owe on credit cards, charge accounts and many loans is bad debt because it doesn't generate income. This debt, which we call the LifeStyle Cycle, depletes your resources and leaves you with less or nothing to invest. In contrast, good debt is acquired through the purchase of assets that produce passive income (income made through your money and investments).

Eliminate your LifeStyle Cycle by completing the five-step debt elimination plan explained in this chapter. Put it down in writing: make a firm, written commitment to eliminate your bad debt and stop creating new consumer debt so you can begin to build your Wealth Cycle.

LORAL'S LEARNING LOOP

What are three things you learned from this chapter?

_____

_____

_____

_____

_____

_____

_____

What three actions will you take as a result of this chapter?

_____

_____

_____

_____

_____

_____

List the dates when you will begin and complete your three actions.

_____

_____

_____

To whom will you be accountable?

_____

_____

GUERRILLA WEALTH

Managing Your Lifestyle Cycle

Building A Wealth Cycle Foundation

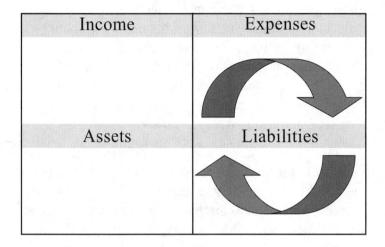

Income	Expenses
Assets	Liabilities

Now it's time to start building your wealth!

The creation of your wealth begins with what we call, "Building Your Wealth Cycles." Everything you've done up to this point has prepared you to build a strong foundation for your financial freedom. The Wealth Cycle is the mechanism – the process – that gets you there.

This is the chapter that takes the mystery out of wealth building. You'll understand how people, even of ordinary means, have become financially free. Finally, it'll blow away any lingering thought that luck has anything to do with becoming wealthy. It's simply a matter of *learning the process* and *getting into action to put the process to work.*

This is another guerrilla wealth tactic that's quite

distinct from the Industrial Age model. A quick historical perspective will be useful to help get your mind around this concept. Wealth Cycles actually reflect the timeless wealth-building reality of thousands of years in the history of man. Up until the late 20th century, people simply couldn't enjoy a lavish lifestyle unless they *first had wealth in place*. And once a family had money, it was easy to keep creating more and more wealth, generation after generation.

On the other hand, workers lived day to day. And there's no question, the harsh reality was that some of the wealthy built their empires on the backs of the working poor. No doubt that's the source of the phrase we still hear repeated, "The rich get richer; the poor get poorer." This is the reason when people see someone accumulating wealth today, many think – perhaps unconsciously – that money was made at the expense of someone else. Somebody won at another's expense.

Yet, even in ancient times, it was possible for a laborer to raise himself up and dramatically improve his life if he could find someone to teach him the principles of the wealthy and began using them. George S. Clason's classic fable, *The Richest Man in Babylon*, shows how even in other times and other cultures – with the exception of dictatorships – the laboring class always has had the key to break free from a cycle of endless, backbreaking work . . . if they used it.

So what happened? In the Industrial Age, the masses had access to work and could achieve The American Dream of owning a home, car and luxuries.

Building A Wealth Cycle Foundation

In the last half of the 20th century, the widespread availability of consumer credit gave people instant access to luxuries *beyond their means*. That gave birth to the LifeStyle Cycles we discussed earlier – earn, spend, earn more, spend more. It became normal to seek a look of affluence far above an individual's actual financial reality.

In a few short years, the wealth-building wisdom of the ages was lost to a majority of individuals who became known simply as "consumers." Consuming became an obsession. Many essentially became indentured servants to creditors. Wealth became an impossible dream.

Enter the Information Age. This is an era of tremendous opportunity. There's money to be made. The truth is, money is already FLOWING through your hands. Once you stop letting it leak out for needless expenses and cut the consumer debt cycle, you have almost unlimited opportunity today to achieve wealth.

In the Information Age we have the choice to live on our own terms. Unlike the centuries past, when few beyond the wealthy knew the principles . . . and unlike the Industrial Age when people foolishly went for the rewards of the rich without actually building wealth first . . . you now have wealth knowledge *and* wisdom at your disposal. Better yet, you live within an economic system that allows – and even encourages – wealth building. Plus, you know there's money you can divert from consuming to wealth building.

There is *nothing* to hold you back. You can earn money guilt-free because in the Information Age, no one has to lose anything for you to win. In fact, "getting your piece of the pie" doesn't even mean there are fewer pieces available. The pie just keeps getting bigger!

This is a fantastic time to build wealth. Your Wealth Cycle is key!

A Wealth Cycle is the process in which:

> ➤ You take your earned money, put it into your wealth account (in your asset column)
> ➤ Invest it well into assets that produce passive income
> ➤ Then re-invest the passive income you make into new assets to produce more consistent passive income

You continue this cycle of turning income into assets, income into assets over and over and over. We call this building "sustainable wealth" because your money is *really, truly working for you* on a continuous basis versus *you working for your money*. Guerrilla Wealth Builders are always focused on having their money work for them and maximizing their rates of return.

Does this just sound too simple to you? Be glad it's this simple because that means you – no matter where you are financially – can do this!

The long-term result of building Wealth Cycles is that it enables you to pass your wealth on for generations. Your wealth will outlive you and allow you to carry on your legacy. The cycle continues as

Building A Wealth Cycle Foundation

long as the assets are managed to produce a healthy rate of return. Guerrilla Wealth Builders focus on the long-term sustainability of their wealth and on being of service to others. They're focused on the larger vision, not just on the here and now or only on themselves.

Like most processes, building a Wealth Cycle must rise from a solid, firmly planted base. Unfortunately, few people create Wealth Cycles, and most of those who do, approach it like a one-time transaction. However, building a Wealth Cycle is a continuous process that you must plan and sustain.

In the previous chapters you've done the work necessary to prepare the ground on which to build your foundation. Now let's begin to build the foundation.

The beginning steps in building a Wealth Cycle foundation are:

> Understanding and utilizing the legal entities which are available to you and the tax implications of each
> Determining whether to be an active or passive investor and beginning to look at the appropriate strategies
> Developing your money rules

These three steps form the foundation of how you will begin to create wealth.

Building A Wealth Cycle Foundation

STEP 1: LEGAL STRUCTURES
AND TAX STRATEGIES

GUERRILLA INTELLIGENCE

If you're an employee, the amount of taxes you pay prevents you from actually making money for yourself until May 10th. So, from January 1st to May 9th, every cent you earn goes to the government in taxes! On May 10th, you begin earning money for yourself!

As almost every expert in the wealth arena will tell you, there are two primary tax structures under U.S. tax laws. The different structures exist for employees and corporations. Employees are taxed on the amounts they earn. Taxes are withheld from employees' paychecks and they get to spend what is left.

Under the corporate tax structure, corporations earn money, deduct all appropriate business deductions, and pay taxes only on the remainder of what is left.

Which would you prefer?

In the United States, a number of legal structures, vehicles or entities may be used to hold and protect your wealth. These structures are separate and distinct from the taxpayers who form and/or own them. When you create any of these entities, the entity is assigned its own Employer Identification Number (EIN), which is separate from your Social Security number. Your

Building A Wealth Cycle Foundation

legal entities are also taxed separately from you personally.

The legal protections and responsibilities differ for each of these vehicles, as do the tax implications. How you structure your investments, and which legal entities you use, can have enormous tax and legal consequences.

Legal business entities are advantageous because they can:

1. Protect your personal assets.
2. Protect you from being held personally liable for legal obligations.
3. Keep your finances and financial dealings private.
4. Maximize your tax savings.

If you're operating a business and you want that business to be treated as your asset and/or you're continuing to grow your business, the legal entity you select can:

1. Protect the entity (i.e., your business).
2. Protect your assets (i.e., your home and other investment real estate; intellectual property, such as trademarks, copyrights, patents and trade secrets).

The goal of asset protection is to minimize your risks and to help grow and maintain your asset base. The right legal entity will provide you with those benefits.

Building A Wealth Cycle Foundation

The following describes the core legal structures available in the United States and the benefits each provide. Outside of the United States, the names may differ, but equivalents exist that operate similarly. The core legal entities in the United States are:

C-Corporation

A C-Corporation is a general for-profit corporation that's required to pay taxes on the income it generates. The "C" refers to the chapter in the U.S. Internal Revenue Service (IRS) Code that governs the corporation's tax reporting. A C-Corporation is a separate legal entity from the shareholders who own its shares. If you form a C-Corporation, in which you own the shares, you can't be held personally liable for the corporation's debts because you and the corporation are separate legal entities. A C-Corporation can furnish goods and services to the general public, own assets, incur liabilities and deduct allowable expenses from its taxes.

When you incorporate your retail store as a C-Corporation, you and the corporation become separate legal entities. If you make all the store's inventory corporate assets, you can't be held personally liable for corporate obligations, even though you own all the corporate shares. Both you and the corporation pay separate taxes, but the corporation is entitled to special tax treatment.

The shareholders of a C-Corporation may elect to

convert the tax reporting status of the corporation to a subchapter S-Corporation, which we'll cover in the next paragraph. Forming a C-Corporation is often the first step in reducing your taxes and protecting your assets. C-Corporations offer approximately 300 tax-deductible expenses. If you want to take your company public, you must first form a C-Corporation. In addition, a C-Corporation's fiscal year can end on either 3/31, 6/30, 9/30 or 12/31, which lets you stagger the due date for taxes. For all other entities, the tax year must end on December 31. Staggering your fiscal years can mean that you don't have such huge tax implications at the end of the year.

S-Corporation

An S-Corporation differs from a C-Corporation because the income it generates is taxed like a partnership or a sole proprietorship. The "S" refers to a different chapter of the IRS Code. In other words, the taxable income earned by the S-Corporation is passed through to its shareholders. Therefore, the S-Corporation doesn't pay taxes, but its shareholders report the income or losses generated by the S-Corporation on their individual tax returns.

An S-Corporation begins its life as a C-Corporation. Its shareholders may elect to switch it to an S-Corporation by filing IRS Form 2553. Some states also require a filing, so check the law in the state in which the C-Corporation was incorporated. By electing to convert to an S-Corporation, you're deciding to have the corporation's earnings treated like a partnership or sole proprietorship income.

Shareholders of S-Corporations are still entitled to protection from liability for claims against the corporation. S-Corporations have approximately 150 allowable expense deductions. They can be used as part of a multi-corporation strategy and with new businesses to decrease your tax liabilities. Losses incurred by S-Corporations also flow through to the shareholders and can reduce their personal tax liability. However, losses incurred by C-Corporations cannot be passed through.

Limited Partnership (LP)

A Limited Partnership must consist of one or more general partners and one or more limited partners. Generally speaking, limited partners share in the Limited Partnership's profits, but are shielded from responsibility for its liabilities. They have no say in the management of the Limited Partnership's activities. In most Limited Partnerships, limited partners are passive financial investors.

A general partner has the benefits and responsibilities of actively managing the Limited Partnership's activities. In exchange, the general partner has unlimited financial and legal responsibility for the Limited Partnership's losses or liabilities. A great way to protect a general partner from unlimited liability is to make the general partner a corporation.

Building A Wealth Cycle Foundation

Limited Partnerships are often used to hold real estate and other investments in which the parties involved don't wish to be on an equal footing. They usually work well when investors want to remain passive and to have someone else (the general partner) manage all of the partnership's business. Limited Partnerships are governed by the content of the partnership agreements they negotiate. Partnership agreements set forth critical information, including percentages of ownership, duties, responsibilities and liabilities.

Family Limited Partnership (FLP)

Simply put, Family Limited Partnerships (FLPs) are limited partnerships in which the majority of the participants are the members of a family. Essentially, they follow the same basic rules (requiring general and limited partners) and enjoy the same benefits of a standard Limited Partnership.

Usually, older family members create FLPs and contribute their assets in exchange for general and limited partnership shares. Limited partnership shares are then given to family members, generally their children and grandchildren. However, the general partners retain control of the FLP. The partnership agreement sets forth how the partnership income is divided.

Although income tax liability passes through to partners automatically, cash isn't distributed to partners until the general partners decide to make distributions. Therefore, the general partners retain control over the FLP's assets and limited partners have restricted rights, including limitations on their ability to transfer their partnership ownership to others.

In an FLP, children under 14 years of age pay no taxes. However, as soon as they turn 14, they take on the tax burden representing their proportional ownership of the FLP. So in a typical FLP, the general partner is a one-percent owner and the kids own all of the rest.

FLPs are powerful vehicles for protecting assets and for estate planning. They can provide substantial tax savings by reducing asset values for estate and gift tax purposes, while they enable the general partners to retain asset control.

Limited Liability Company (LLC)

A Limited Liability Company (LLC) is the newest of all entities. For tax purposes, an LLC is not a separate taxable entity, but LLC owners, who are called members, report business gains or losses on their personal income tax returns. LLC members are protected from personal liability for LLC debts except to the extent of their investment in the LLC. An LLC can be formed with just one member in all states except for Massachusetts, which requires two members. (Each state annually changes the regulations for entity structures. Be sure to consult with an attorney or CPA for current information.)

Building A Wealth Cycle Foundation

Unlike the partners in a Limited Partnership, LLC members are all on an equal footing. Therefore, all LLC members have the opportunity to actively participate in the LLC's activities. Although LLCs are a newer legal entity, they've been around long enough to be time-tested. LLCs are great vehicles for holding real estate and other investments, especially for individuals who want to limit their personal liability.

Trusts

A Trust is a legal structure that is used to hold legal title to property for the benefit of one or more persons. The individual who creates the Trust is known as the Trust Creator or Grantor. The person or institution holding legal title to the property is called the Trustee, and the people who are intended to benefit from the Trust are known as Beneficiaries.

If you put assets in a trust for your minor children to receive when they each become 21 years old, you're the Trust Creator or Grantor. Your children are the Beneficiaries and your brother is the Trustee – if he holds the legal title to the property.

Trusts are powerful vehicles for several reasons. First, they place the property in a separate entity that's outside the reach of creditors. This prevents your creditors from getting access to your assets to satisfy your debts. Second, they can be used to pass property to others tax-free. At this time, the government allows $2 million in trust funds to go to a beneficiary's estate tax free, but that amount will gradually increase to $10 million in 2010. Finally, they take the property outside the reach of beneficiaries who may have insatiable financial appetites.

With a trust, you can redirect monies to others by giving them gifts from income generated by the assets. So, if you want to give a loved one a gift, but are unsure of their ability to properly manage it, a trust may be the perfect solution.

GUERRILLA INTELLIGENCE

Visualize legal entities as if they were a bucket in which you put like-type assets.

➤ One bucket, a limited liability company (LLC), may hold several of the rental properties you own;

➤ A second bucket, an LLC, might hold your software business and all its inventory;

➤ A third bucket, a partnership, may contain your patents for auto parts; and

➤ A fourth bucket, a sub-chapter C-Corporation, may manage your real estate holdings.

Your buckets operate as organizational tools to hold like-type assets. They keep them separate from your other assets, protect those assets, and provide you with a great tax strategy and benefits.

Building A Wealth Cycle Foundation

Legal entities that pass through taxes can provide business continuity upon your death. So, if your business is in a trust, an LLC or an S-Corporation, it can continue without interruption after you die.

MAXIMIZING TAX STRATEGIES

In our experience, most business owners and investors don't properly utilize legitimate business deductions; they pay too many deductible business expenses from their personal funds. This failure frequently costs them substantial money that they could be putting back into their business or investing to increase their wealth.

The following list identifies some of the typical business expenses that you can deduct to minimize your tax burden. You must have a legal business structure in place in order to take advantage of these deductions. Also, each entity has its own guidelines and legal specifications that determine what can be deducted and for how much.

Some examples of business deductions are:

➤ Utilities
➤ Entertainment
➤ Automobile
➤ Insurance
➤ Computer equipment
➤ Rent (office or home office deduction)
➤ Phone

Building A Wealth Cycle Foundation

- ➤ Meals
- ➤ Gas
- ➤ Office supplies
- ➤ Employees
- ➤ Education
- ➤ Travel
- ➤ DSL/Internet service
- ➤ Legal fees
- ➤ Accounting/bookkeeping fees
- ➤ Contractors
- ➤ Websites
- ➤ Marketing
- ➤ Bonuses/Incentives
- ➤ Coaches
- ➤ Education
- ➤ Corporate housing
- ➤ Gifts

. . . and the list goes on and on. In fact, the IRS code specifies over 150 deductions for an S-Corp and 300 deductions for a C-Corp.

IMPORTANT

Consult with your financial advisor, CPA or tax strategist to ensure you're claiming the maximum amount of deductions, or hire a Live Out Loud Coach. For a FREE Incorporation and Tax Strategy, contact: info@liveoutloud.com or call 888-262-2402.

Building A Wealth Cycle Foundation

In the space below, list those deductions that you may not be fully utilizing:

_____

_____

_____

_____

_____

_____

_____

If you have any questions regarding these items, contact us at info@liveoutloud.com.

No matter what your tax situation, proper documentation is the key to maximizing your tax strategies and getting all of your allowable tax deductions. This entails maintaining precise accounting records. If you wish to deduct the cost of an item from your taxes, you must be able to justify the deduction by producing the following information for each deduction:

1. The exact cost of the item, not a guess.
2. The date of purchase.
3. A description of the purchase. For example, a marketing dinner for a client, supplies for rental real estate properties or gas for a business trip.
4. The business purpose of the purchase.

Building A Wealth Cycle Foundation

Based on the information you've learned in this chapter, what are some of the action steps that you plan to take to protect your business?

They could be to:

1.   Have an incorporation strategy session,
2.   Have your current tax plan reviewed, or
3.   Meet with a trust attorney.

List your action step plans below:

_____

_____

_____

_____

_____

_____

_____

_____

STEP 2: ACTIVE OR PASSIVE INVESTING

Before you decide on the investment strategies you plan to follow, determine whether you want to be an active or passive investor. Active investors get directly involved in the investment. They may become general partners or take roles in the management of a business or particular venture. In contrast, a passive investor

Building A Wealth Cycle Foundation

essentially only puts up money, sits back, lets others do the work and waits for profits to come in.

Investors seldom decide beforehand whether they wish to invest actively or passively. If you don't decide, however, the decision may be made for you by default. For example, your stockbroker could make trades or your property manager could make decisions without consulting you. Alternatively, you could be called upon to contribute time, energy and expertise to enterprises that don't interest you.

If you don't have a solid investment plan that you lead and control, you could fall prey to unscrupulous individuals who need investor money for questionable deals. Many of these operators are polished and sophisticated. They're experts in luring investors into get-rich-quick schemes that sound "too good to be true," a cliché that in investing is, unfortunately, frequently true.

Most important, if you haven't decided whether to be an active or passive investor, you haven't fully thought through what your investing strategies should be. As a result, you could be forced to react to opportunities, rather than being in a position to pro-actively focus your investment strategies on making lucrative deals. When you fully plan your approaches, you can make things happen. When you don't, you have to sit, wait, and then make the best out of what you get. This is the "park and pray" process we mentioned earlier. It doesn't work.

Building A Wealth Cycle Foundation

Considerations when making the decision of active vs. passive control of your investment:

Do you enjoy the process of investing in your particular niche?

_____

How much time and energy would you like to commit?

_____

Are you willing to confront the necessary learning curve?

_____

_____

How much control are you willing to give others if you don't have the necessary time?

_____

_____

How much responsibility are you willing to take for the results of your investments?

_____

_____

List other considerations that might affect your investment or participation:

_____

Building A Wealth Cycle Foundation

Every decision on investments and investment strategies must be based on your unique objectives, values and circumstances. There is no one size or "fits all" strategy. What financial outcomes do you want, cash, equity or cash flow? If wealth is your objective, select the strategy that seems best for you and look for opportunities in which that strategy will help you get rich.

GUERRILLA TACTIC

WARNING: If you decide to become an active investor, be prepared to face a serious learning curve. It may take you considerable time and effort to get up to speed and to reach the level where you can help a venture make money.

The purpose of this warning is not to deter you, but to make sure that you're realistic and prepared for how much work you may have to undertake. To help you succeed and gain the necessary knowledge you'll need more quickly, we encourage you to approach investing as a team sport.

Identify and partner with top people who know what they're doing and whose strengths complement your shortcomings. Find experts who can teach you and help you cover all the bases. Become part of an investment group in which you invest on your own, but learn and succeed as a team.

So, how should you decide?

Building A Wealth Cycle Foundation

Active	Passive
Day trading	Give your money to a broker and let them trade for you
Real Estate - Finding properties and working with an active team	401K / Pension Plan
Actively running a business	Giving your money to a real estate team—letting them manage it as an asset
Analyzing private placement memorandums (PPMs)	Investing in a partnership but you have a silent role.

When you decide whether to be an active or passive investor, your decision will propel your investing strategy. It'll color the way you see, find and approach opportunities. Simply making the decision will sharpen your focus and open you up to fascinating new people and information. Better yet, it will enable you to begin to **Accelerate Your Wealth Cycles**.

STEP 3: MONEY RULES

In building the foundation for your Wealth Cycle, you now have two steps in place: (1) you've established the most beneficial legal entity with the best tax strategy, and (2) you know whether you'll be a passive or active investor. Now, you have one final step to complete to assure a solid foundation: you must decide upon and commit to your money rules.

Money rules are your rules. They are the financial principles you have strategically determined will ensure that you stay on track with your wealth plan.

We all have money rules, each and every one of us! Our rules have either supported us to get where we are right now, or have completely sabotaged our results. Our current money rules determine how we handle money, think about wealth and run our finances.

We encourage you to set very specific, pre-determined rules designed to support you to stay in the conversation about money. Make the appropriate decisions and take the right actions to create the results you want in your wealth plan.

Examples of money rules may be:

➢ Pay yourself first into your wealth account.
➢ Never use your wealth account for anything but assets.
➢ Pay off your credit cards monthly.
➢ Maintain a monthly forecast.
➢ Stay out of consumer debt.
➢ Modify your strategy as the economy changes.

In the space provided, please list the money rules that you follow:

_____

_____

_____

Building A Wealth Cycle Foundation

Read each rule you listed and ask yourself:

(1) Does this work for me?

(2) What is the result that I want from it?

1. _____

_____

_____

2. _____

_____

_____

Regardless of what your past experience has been, set money rules now that will be absolutely **non-negotiable!** Setting non-negotiable rules is mandatory for your financial success.

If the concept of money rules is new to you, you may not have the knowledge needed to make some of your rules non-negotiable at this time. However, you soon will if you continue to educate yourself about each of the investment strategies you're considering. If you stay focused on your goals and are flexible, your money rules will clearly evolve.

SUCCESS STORIES

Jason Stewardson

Before I met Loral, I had bought about 30 houses and held all as rentals. Unfortunately, I'd reached the point where banks wouldn't loan me more money and I was losing lots of money. The fact that all 30 houses were in my name wasn't helping me with taxes either. In January 2003, I joined Loral's Big Table. By the end of 2004, I will have borrowed over $1.5 million and doubled my rental houses from 30 to 60. Now, banks are eager to issue me lines of credit to buy more property.

I was able to reverse my financial situation because Loral taught me how to create a solid wealth foundation. Before joining her Big Table, I was trying to stack a bunch of stuff on top of nothing. She taught me to take three steps to build my foundation: (1) Change my psychology about money, including where to get it and how I think about it. (2) Raise private funds – using other people's money is good for me and for them. (3) Take everything out of my name. Now, I have six different LLCs that own properties and an S-corporation that manages them.

Thanks to Loral, I now pay my investors an eight to ten percent return on their investment. I'm able to start an LLC, use my investors' capital to buy 10 to 15 houses, then go to the bank and get a loan. As a result, I came out of it with between $20,000 and $50,000 in cash per LLC. Last week, I closed a deal that brought in almost $40,000. With my lines of credit, I plan to move into purchasing apartments and multi-family residences."

Jim Neville

"Loral helped me fulfill my dream. When I first heard her speak six years ago, I was working with a non-profit agency for kids and was very much in debt. She taught me how to set up a company that would work. After working with Loral, I started Life School, which takes kids on backpacking trips, sea kayaking, and other outdoor adventures. I now do what I love and Loral was my first board member.

Life School is now four years old and I'm making over $100,000 in revenue, and have served over 1,000 kids. Last year, after taking Loral's advice on investing in myself, I changed how I marketed the business, tripling its revenue in one year. By thinking of Life School as a true business and creating high-quality marketing materials, I increased its fundraising revenue by over 150 percent in a single year.

I learned that a non-profit doesn't have to be broke, so I run Life School like a business and hire quality staff. Loral taught me that to succeed, you must create your own marketing, sell to donors, build a great team and take full ownership of your life. You can't expect others to come to your rescue. Success is a result of what you do with the information you get.

By taking care of me first and building the business foundation, my psychology about money went from 'not enough' to knowing that plenty of resources exist. People do not lack resources, they only lack ambition or motivation. I can find any answer to any problem. It exists. It's just a matter of searching it out."

SUMMING UP

A number of legal structures or entities can be used to hold and protect your wealth. These entities are separate from the taxpayers who form and/or own them. They include corporations (such as C-Corporations and S-Corporations), Limited Partnerships, Family Limited Partnerships, Limited Liability Companies and Trusts. Each entity has specific advantages and disadvantages. Two of the most important advantages are that they may limit your personal liability and provide you with tax benefits.

Before settling on your investment strategies, decide if you will be an active or passive investor. Active investors get directly involved in the investment, while passive investors usually put up the money, letting others do the work and collect the profits.

Also, commit to non-negotiable money rules, a group of financial principles that you will live by. If you stay focused on your goals and remain flexible, your money rules will continue to evolve based on the economic conditions and your goals.

LORAL'S LEARNING LOOP

What are three things you learned from this chapter?

_____

_____

_____

_____

_____

What three actions will you take as a result of this chapter?

_____

_____

_____

_____

_____

List the dates when you will begin and complete your three actions.

_____

_____

_____

To whom will you be accountable?

_____

Section III

YOUR
WEALTH
ACCELERATION

7

Acceleration of Your Wealth Cycles

*"Wealth accumulates when your money
is working for you
instead of when you're working for your money.
It builds systematically over time."*

Do you think building a foundation for wealth is exciting? Wait until you learn how to get your money working harder than you ever imagined!

It might surprise you to know that just one percent of the world's population truly understands the REAL secrets of affluence. Those who are willing to share their knowledge usually provide only concepts, not the detailed "how to" that you need to create wealth.

We'll tell you what you need to know! This is where we move you into an entirely different level of financial freedom. Accelerating your Wealth Cycles takes you from financial security to sustainable wealth. This is when your wealth account becomes your personal money-making machine.

One of the great advantages of investing now – in the Information Age – is simply that we have more information. Opportunities that used to be reserved for a small, knowledgeable group of professionals and their elite investors are now available to you. Even better, information is no longer hidden behind the closed doors of brokerage firms and other financial institutions. You have the ability to find out almost anything you need to know on the Internet. It's the greatest research tool available to investors. Best of all, the Information Age itself has spawned many new companies, emerging industries and global opportunities never available before.

Accelerating your Wealth Cycles employs a full range of guerrilla tactics. Just because these tactics aren't commonly used in the mainstream doesn't mean you should shy away from them. In fact, this is one place where *not* following the crowd can be the most profitable choice of all. We personally use these techniques. Our clients, even those with little previous financial expertise, are using them today. Though aggressive, these investment opportunities are anything but close to the edge legally or dangerously risky. So pay close attention.

Before you can take advantage of the guerrilla tactics used for accelerating Wealth Cycles, you need to have gone through the process described in the earlier chapters of this book:

1. Know your financial conditioning or mindset and modify accordingly.
2. Know your financial baseline.
3. Create and implement your forecast.
4. Set your Financial Freedom Day.
5. Know and have control over your LifeStyle Cycle.
6. Create your Wealth Cycle foundation to include corporate structure.

If you haven't completed these first six steps, you'll

be building on a foundation that's not solid. You won't be able to accelerate your Wealth Cycle. You may be able to spot deals and opportunities – and you may even close a few – but if your system isn't up and running, your options will be severely limited. You'll miss out on great investment opportunities. Even worse, you may see your financial foundation crumble underneath you.

GUERRILLA INTELLIGENCE

Many definitions of wealth exist. It's been defined as "a great quantity of valuable material, possessions or resources."

For our purposes, wealth is the accumulation of assets. When invested well, your assets produce a consistent flow of passive income. The point you want to reach is when your assets work for you to produce more and more lucrative assets.

WHEN TO ACCELERATE

One of the first questions you'll face is, "When should I start to accelerate my investing?"

As soon as you have your Wealth Cycle foundation in place. The sooner, the better.

History shows that, over time, successful investors

began investing when they were young. Their average age was 24 when they made their first investment.

Investing is a lifelong process that you should begin as early as possible and manage throughout your life. It's the process of continually building your asset pool, and as you become more sophisticated, you'll reallocate those assets to get higher and higher returns. If, however, you're starting late, don't be discouraged. You aren't disqualified from playing simply because you didn't start early.

> *"The eighth wonder of the world is*
> *the compounding power of money."*
> Albert Einstein

GUERRILLA TACTIC

Since the world is constantly changing, be prepared to change too, and to reallocate portions of your portfolio accordingly. When interest rates are low, it can be a great time to borrow. When interest is high, it might be smart to lend.

When your needs and desires change, your investment strategy must be flexible enough to follow suit and meet new conditions and demands. Flexibility is an asset and many investors will pay a premium for it. The ability to make quick, well-reasoned changes has value and will help you to confidently take charge of your investment strategy in spite of changes that occur.

Acceleration of Your Wealth Cycles

Every investment plan is different. We believe that financial coaching and mentoring on a one-on-one basis are essential in order to look at your particular situation and to understand your individual financial fingerprint. We can then help you build the right strategy, and the ideal investing plan for you and the life you want to create.

So how do you decide when to invest? Get educated. Find a mentor. As Loral always says:

"Reading will give you knowledge.

Action will give you experience.

Results will give you confidence."

There are many ways to educate yourself about investment strategies:

1. Read investment and finance books.
2. Find a mentor. Choose someone who is successful and who will share his or her experiences with you.
3. Read the financial sections of newspapers daily. Develop an understanding of the language and the developments reported in the news.
4. Subscribe to and read financial and investment newsletters and magazines, online and in print.
5. Watch TV and listen to radio finance and investment programs.

Acceleration of Your Wealth Cycles

6.   Hire professional wealth team members.
7.   Attend courses, lectures, workshops and seminars.
8.   Speak with colleagues and build financial and investment networks.
9.   Join investment groups, clubs or organizations.

HOW WILL YOU INVEST?

Since investments aren't the primary income source for some people, they tend to approach investing as if it were something extra that doesn't warrant their full involvement. They treat it as a one-time transaction or as a process that someone else, such as a financial planner, CPA, banker, mate or parent, should manage. That's a huge mistake!

Your main job in creating wealth is to confidently take the lead in directing your wealth plan. You can't turn this important role over to anyone else, for some very good reasons:

> ➢ **NO ONE** will look after your investments as well as you.
> ➢ **NO ONE** will care about your investments as much as you.
> ➢ **NO ONE** will give your investments as much attention as you.
> ➢ **NO ONE** will understand your investing objectives as well as you.
> ➢ **NO ONE** will have as much to lose as you.

Acceleration of Your Wealth Cycles

In many areas, others will have greater knowledge, more experience and better insights than you – at least at first. You may even face a steep learning curve. Therefore, you must learn and work to gain that knowledge, experience and insight.

We also know that most successful investors:

➢ Invested small amounts of money CONSISTENTLY, year by year, until they accumulated larger amounts. They continually invested their profits and added additional money to their accounts when possible.
➢ Invested often. 92 percent of successful investors added to their investment choices monthly.
➢ Invested intelligently. 81 percent earmarked money for emergency funds and then accelerated the amount they invested each month. They also consistently allocated their funds to diverse assets.

GUERRILLA INTELLIGENCE

The bottom line is that investing your money and assets is YOUR role. If you're serious about accumulating wealth, your number one job is to CONFIDENTLY TAKE CHARGE OF YOUR WEALTH PLAN. You're the commander-in-chief, the boss and the head honcho – so the buck stops with you.

> **GUERRILLA INTELLIGENCE** (cont'd)
>
> Learn about investing and gain experience so you can make the essential decisions and not leave them to others. Sure, it's important to always get the best expert advice. However, even if you're being advised by Warren Buffett, Alan Greenspan or Paul Allen, the final decisions about how to invest your funds are up to you.

Investing successfully requires:

1. Learning
2. Experiencing
3. Enduring
4. Diversifying
5. Leading.

Learning is the process of acquiring knowledge about the areas that you plan to enter. It involves finding out about investments and mastering those areas in which you wish to invest. For example, you may have to gather information about a regional real estate market, local property values, occupancy rates, current rental ranges, mortgage terms or management costs.

Experiencing is the process of doing it, and of going through the trial and error of learning the practical aspects of your areas of interest. It's the hands-on contact that teaches you how the nuts and bolts of your investments work. Experience also enables you to understand which people you can count on, and to get to know their strengths, weaknesses and values.

Acceleration of Your Wealth Cycles

Enduring is being patient and creating long-term plans, not just quickies. To build Wealth Cycles, investment strategies can't be hit and run. They must be consistent parts of an overall program designed in detail to bring you wealth. Since economies tend to run in cycles, your investments will hit bumps and potholes along the way. So you must plan for, and position yourself, to make the best of surprises and tough times.

Diversifying is the art of investing in many opportunities, rather than just one or two investments. Diversification sounds simple enough, so why is its implementation so difficult? Usually, it's because of your old conditioning. Remember that some of the best-laid investing plans can easily be destroyed by bad, out-of-date psychology. Failure to diversify is also the product of a LACK of mastering the other investing elements: learning, experiencing, enduring and leading.

Leading means that you don't have to do it all yourself. Create wealth by assembling a team of experts who can help you reach your goals, and then lead that team. Leading your wealth team will be covered in detail in the following chapter.

DIVERSIFICATION

The key to diversifying your investments is asset allocation: investing in different types of assets. Most wealthy people invest in a wide range of asset classes. They're always looking for purchases that will provide strong returns and will consider opportunities in many areas.

Although many investors concentrate on particular fields, they usually diversify within their field. They identify a number of investments in that area and select those they feel will perform best. Your financial tools and investment choices include:

> ## Cash & Cash Equivalents
> Cash. We like to have cash or the equivalents because they're safe and very liquid. Examples of cash equivalents include checks, negotiable money orders, bank account balances, Treasury Bills and money market funds. Your wealth account would be in this category: money readily available to invest on a moment's notice.

> ## Bonds
> These are simple certificates of debt issued to raise money for a government or corporation. Bonds promise to pay a specific sum – typically the principal plus interest – at a fixed rate on a specific date in the future. Bonds come in many forms, including corporate bonds, municipal bonds, treasury bonds, notes or bills, and zero-coupon bonds. Bonds are rated according to risk of default. Should a company default on a bond, the bondholder has priority over shareholders in the distribution of assets.

Acceleration of Your Wealth Cycles

➤ **Stocks**
A stock is a financial instrument that indicates ownership in a corporation and a proportionate share of the corporation's assets and profits. Stockholders are also known as shareholders.

➤ **Real Estate**
Real estate is, simply, a piece of land that includes the space above that land, the ground below it, and any buildings or structures located on it.

➤ **International Securities**
These are securities which are sold in a number of national markets at the same time by a syndicate.

➤ **Precious Metals**
Investors interested in precious metals are buying gold, silver, platinum and palladium.

➤ **Natural Resources**
Investors are generally interested in oil and gas, coal, water or land.

➤ **Commodities**
In commodities trading, the investor is buying or selling, usually through futures contracts which designate specified prices to be paid on specified future dates. Commodities include agricultural products such as grain or other food products, or metals.

> **Collectibles**
Antiques and rare objects can dramatically increase in value. The disadvantage is that the investment isn't liquid, and it may be difficult to find a buyer willing to pay the value when the investor wants to sell.

> **Businesses**
Investing in a business provides an investor the opportunity to branch out into a variety of industries.

This is only an overview to introduce you to the key investing opportunities. Each has an upside and a downside. Commit now to become an educated investor by reading, attending classes or seminars, and tapping the expertise of financial advisors or coaches.

In Chapter 6, *Building A Wealth Cycle Foundation*, we introduced you to the concept of control as it applied to active and passive investments. Now let's examine the concept of control and diversification further. The graphic below is a bulls-eye that depicts control and diversification.

Acceleration of Your Wealth Cycles

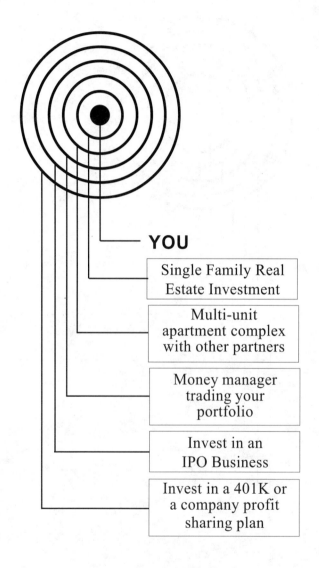

In the space provided on the following page, determine what your diversification of assets will be based on the amount of control you desire.

Acceleration of Your Wealth Cycles

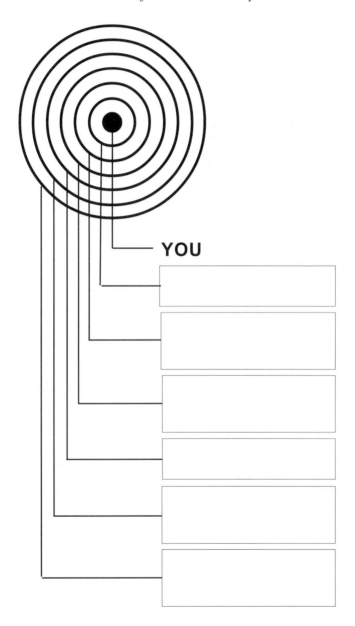

YOU

Acceleration of Your Wealth Cycles

When you decide to diversify your investments, consider how much activity and control will be involved in each investment. As you can see from the chart above:

> ➤ The more investments you have in the inner circle, the higher degree of control you must exert. In other words, the more active you must be.
> ➤ On the other hand, the further your investments are from the target, the less control you can exert. Since your out-of-target investments require less control, they will be more passive.

The guerrilla wealth strategy is to build a portfolio that contains a *diverse blend of assets* that will give you the *highest amount of control*. If you create a diverse portfolio, you won't be married to any single investment type, so your purchases will be based on potential returns and less influenced by subjective factors. In addition, if you diversify, you won't be as badly burnt when a particular category hits a bump, as most investments do.

To control a diverse portfolio, YOU MUST LEAD YOUR WEALTH TEAM. It's essential for you to work with others because you can't do it all expertly by yourself. We'll discuss leadership more in the next chapter, but for now, let's continue getting your investment plan in place.

Let's examine the asset classes previously discussed in greater detail, according to the model that we modified from Ric Edelman's book, *Ordinary People, Extraordinary Wealth* (HarperBusiness, 2000). As you examine them, see how many investment options you have and determine if these choices can provide you with high levels of investment creativity.

Stocks
 ➢ Large Cap Vs. Small Cap

Commodities
 ➢ Options
 ➢ Futures

Natural Resources
 ➢ Minerals
 ➢ Oil and Gas
 ➢ Lumber and Paper

Precious Metals
 ➢ Gold
 ➢ Silver
 ➢ Platinum

International Securities
 ➢ Stocks
 ➢ Bonds
 ➢ Global vs. Continental vs. Nation-Specific

Acceleration of Your Wealth Cycles

Growth vs. Value

> ➢ Specific Industry Sectors (such as technology, financial services, airline, pharmaceuticals, automotive, oil/gas, etc)

Real Estate

> ➢ Residential
>> Buy & Hold
>> Cash - Flips
>> Cashflow
> ➢ Commercial
> ➢ Speculative (raw land)

Collectibles

> ➢ Stamps
> ➢ Coins
> ➢ Gemstones
> ➢ Artwork
> ➢ Sports Memorabilia
> ➢ Other Collectibles

Cash and Cash Equivalents

> ➢ Savings Accounts
> ➢ Checking Accounts
> ➢ Money Market Accounts
> ➢ Certificates of Deposit
> ➢ U.S. Treasury Bills & EE Savings Bonds

Bonds

 ➤ U.S. Government & Agency Securities
 ➤ Municipal Bonds
 ➤ High Quality Corporate Bonds
 ➤ High-yield (junk) Bonds

Business

 ➤ PPM (Private Placement Memorandum)
 ➤ IPO (Initial Public Offering)

How you diversify your assets is a personal decision that will depend on you and your own unique situation. Many people will question how a diverse portfolio should look. What percent of what kind of assets should be included in your portfolio? The guerrilla investor puts more non-traditional assets into the portfolio. The following are examples of a few Guerrilla Wealth Asset Allocation plans:

Example #1

 Real Estate – 30 percent
 Stock Market – 20 percent
 Gas & Oil – 10 percent
 Cash – 10 percent
 Businesses – 30 percent

Example #2

 Real Estate Business – 60 percent
 Stock Market – 20 percent
 Gas & Oil – 10 percent
 Cash – 10 percent

Example #3
Real Estate – 20 percent
Stock Market – 50 percent
Cash – 5 percent
Businesses – 25 percent

Improve your chances of making wise decisions by assembling a top-notch wealth team and getting expert help and advice. Work with the best people you can; there's no substitute for great talent. We'll share more about this in the next chapter.

RISK - REWARD FORMULA

They say you must risk more in order to be rewarded more. Risk is aligned with education. Smart investors risk little because they're well educated about the marketplace and stay connected with their communities. They can read the numbers and know what could be a good investment. For real estate investments, savvy investors look at the numbers first, and if they check out, they then look at the property.

Growing your wealth is an educational process. As you build wealth, you'll develop new understanding and learn how to vary your strategy according to the investment climate and your particular needs and circumstances.

Some people may have to invest more in order to obtain comparable results. For one person, a $50,000 investment may not represent much risk, but for another, it could be his or her last dime. Similarly, the identical return on an investment can have a far greater impact on a young couple who are just starting out than it would on a billionaire in a different tax bracket.

When it comes to risk, remember these rules. Smart investors:

> - Risk little. Whenever possible, they operate with other people's money and spend as little of their own as possible.
> - Are educated and strategic in the marketplace. They study their markets, get expert advice and don't take reckless gambles.
> - Tend to become experts in specific investment areas and specialize within those areas. They learn how to diversify their investments in their specialty fields.
> - Maintain detailed and complete records.
> - Understand how to read and calculate numbers to analyze investment opportunities.
> - Have money rules that they follow.
> - Lead and communicate with their wealth teams.

Smart investors build wealth by using their assets to generate more assets. They may start with a business and use the profits from that business to fund an investment, such as real estate. Then they'll combine the return from their real estate venture along with money from their business to invest in stocks, bonds, or oil and gas leases. In the process, they're diversifying their portfolios and may end up with as many as 10 to 20 legal entities that own their investments. Smart investors also have non-negotiable money rules they follow.

Acceleration of Your Wealth Cycles

When you think about your Wealth Cycle acceleration and your asset allocation, what do you want in your portfolio? Let's design your asset column for wealth. Start by asking yourself, what types of assets will you purchase, how much are you going to invest and what are the expected returns? Enter your answers in the chart that follows.

This following exercise is to get you started thinking properly about the acceleration of your wealth. To complete the excercise, list the asset type that you would like in your wealth portfolio, the amount you will invest and your expected return, based on the money rules you set earlier. We expect that you will consult with your professional wealth team before making an investment. An uninformed or impulsive investment is not the same as being decisive or bold.

Asset Type	Amount Invested	Expected Returns

Acceleration of Your Wealth Cycles

As you plan to accelerate your wealth, don't forget the basic principles, such as your money rules, how much you're willing to risk, and old, unworkable concepts you need to change. Always keep them in mind. Now, reinforce those basic concepts by answering the following questions.

1. What money rules will support your investment decisions?

_____

_____

_____

_____

_____

_____

_____

_____

2. What information do you need to confirm your initial decision?

_____

_____

_____

_____

_____

_____

3. How much are you willing to risk? What is your
    tolerance for loss?

    _____

    _____

    _____

    _____

    _____

    _____

4. What thinking must you change to support your
    investment choices?

    _____

    _____

    _____

    _____

    _____

    _____

5. What must you do today?

    _____

    _____

    _____

    _____

    _____

Acceleration of Your Wealth Cycles

Successful investors follow a plan that allows them to learn more, and be mentored and coached. As a reader of *Guerrilla Wealth*, you're entitled to a free Action Strategy Session with one of the Live Out Loud strategists (valued at over $150). To schedule your free session, call 1-888-262-2402.

6. What will you read? List books, magazines and other investment materials that you will read on a regular basis.

Books:

_____

_____

Magazines:

_____

_____

Newspapers:

_____

_____

Newsletters (print and online):

_____

_____

_____

Acceleration of Your Wealth Cycles

7. Who will be your mentor? Select someone more successful than you who plays a bigger and better game than you play. Loral Langemeier can be your personal mentor through participation in Loral's Big Table—www.loralsbigtable.com.

---

8. Who will be your coach and hold you accountable for the actions that you commit yourself to complete? Loral Langemeier's team of Master Coaches can start you on your path—www.lolcoaching.com.

** We encourage you to ALWAYS seek financial advice from a professional, certified expert. Consult your CPA for tax implications on all investments AND always be certain to align your team with your strategy for wealth-building. The responsibility for acquiring wealth is yours.

CHARITABLE CONTRIBUTIONS

For every wealth plan, we encourage you to donate a percentage of your wealth toward gifting or charitable contributions. Community and generosity are substantial components of wealth. As you acquire more, help those in need – it's enormously rewarding.

Live Out Loud's charity of choice is LifeSchool. You can visit this phenomenal program at http://www.life-school.org.

List your gifting/tithing/contribution rules.

_____

_____

_____

_____

_____

SUCCESS STORIES

Jeff Moody

"When I met Loral in November of 2002, I had been looking at a lot of financial stuff, taking various seminars and programs. I knew I had to change my thinking about money, but I didn't know how to systematize it and move forward. Loral taught me about accountability: I not only had to start taking risks, I had to find ways to be held accountable. The idea is that when you tell someone else about your plans, it ramps it up to another level.

Prior to my working with Loral, my medical practice was operating in the red. At Loral's urging, I systemized my business. It increased my passive income from $2,000 to $6,500 in 18 months and increased my business revenue by 50 percent. And, I'm on schedule to boost it by another 30 percent in three years. Loral is all about systems. If you have a good system, the system will catch you if you start to fail. A good system will also keep you moving forward.

Very little of wealth has to do with income or bank statements, but it has everything to do with your mind and how you think about wealth. The Big Table alters in a positive way the way you think about money, your psychology about money and the psychology about how you relate to money. Once my psychology about money started to change, my credit card bills went away. The amount of money I was able to invest radically increased – with the same amount of income. I started making different choices and set different priorities.

In six months, I went from not being able to pay my bills to putting $20,000 into real estate investments. Add to that the almost $100,000 that I'll save next year through some smart entity structuring, creating a group purchasing organization and other complex maneuvers. It all starts and ends with being accountable, building a great team and taking calculated risks."

SUMMING UP

Your main job in creating wealth is to confidently lead your wealth plan. Investing successfully requires learning, experiencing, enduring, diversifying and leading. Acquire knowledge about your investments, and get experience by actually investing. Be patient. Fortunes are not built overnight, although with guerrilla wealth tactics, wealth can accelerate very fast. Purchase a wide range of diverse money-making investments and surround yourself with the best, most knowledgeable experts available.

Smart investors build wealth by using their assets to generate more assets. Visualize the specific types of assets you would like your investment portfolio to contain. As you plan to accelerate your wealth, stay focused on the basics: your money rules, getting detailed information before you invest, deciding how much you're willing to risk, knowing what thinking you must change to support your investment choices and determining what you must do today.

LORAL'S LEARNING LOOP

What are three things you learned from this chapter?

_____

_____

_____

_____

_____

_____

_____

_____

_____

Acceleration of Your Wealth Cycles

What three actions will you take as a result of this chapter?

_____

_____

_____

_____

_____

_____

List the dates when you will begin and complete your three actions.

_____

_____

_____

To whom will you be accountable?

_____

_____

8

Leadership of Your Wealth Team

*"Leadership is the capacity and will
to rally men and women
to a common purpose and the
character which inspires confidence."*
Bernard Montgomery,
British Field Marshal

Now it's time to learn how to take command and lead your wealth team!

This is yet another fairly new concept for most people, so let's get rid of the leftover Industrial Age ideas that could slow you down. In the Industrial Age, the truly great wealthy industrialists knew how to lead their teams. They knew they didn't have to know everything.

Unfortunately, most were married to the concept of "being the Boss," and that carried over into all their relationships. Everyone was considered a subordinate.

Here's a wake-up call. In the Information Age, all teams are peer-to-peer teams. Within corporations, for example, teams form and Bob is the leader for Project A, but when the team works on Project B, Ellen is the team leader.

The dynamic is entirely different. Today, everyone needs to know how to be a good leader as well as a follower to accommodate this new, more fluid way of doing business. But in your wealth-building efforts, you're the leader. Period. This doesn't give you an ounce of permission to revert to the old "do what I say because I say it" routine.

Today you lead through inspiration. People love to work with people going places. People are starved for the energy and excitement that business was always meant to have. Help your team catch your vision. Believe us when we tell you it's the fun and excitement, even more than the money, that keeps our own wealth teams completely engaged with us. And by the way, we're the same with other people and their dreams. It's not just about our own deals. It's about all of us, together.

But let's talk about why you need a wealth team. When it comes to wealth-building, you can't do everything yourself. Far too much is involved and the Lone Rangers, who try to do it themselves, disappeared with the Industrial Age. That's why you must assemble a top-flight wealth team and learn to lead it well.

The reality is, in today's complex, fast-paced world of business, few people have the time or talent to do everything expertly themselves even if they want to. You may be the most far-seeing visionary, brilliant dealmaker, toughest negotiator and finest closer, but are you also an inspired strategist, a tax wizard, a legal genius or a great manager?

Leadership of Your Wealth Team

THE BEST

Recruit the best experts to give you strategic advice. Some members of your team may already be in place: your accountant, lawyer and stockbroker. Now start thinking about filling in your team. One of the biggest problems we find in wealth building is that people tend to hold back and wait until they feel they "need" expert advice. That is, when they have some wealth to worry about.

Our guerrilla approach is exactly opposite of that thinking. To finish well, you need to start well. The time you really need superior advice and expert coaching is in the early stages of building your wealth. A good team can keep you from making mistakes that cost you time and money while you're in the learning curve. You don't want to wait until later to discover you've needlessly wasted thousands on taxes or innocently bought a stock or property with a fatal flaw that a professional would have spotted in a minute.

Even if you're just starting out on your journey to wealth, your objective is to build and lead the best, world-class, top-flight wealth team. You don't have to hire them all now, but start identifying who you need and how you can connect with them. In constructing your wealth team, surround yourself with the best and the smartest. You should not be the smartest and most expert member of your team.

In the beginning, the best may be difficult to afford or even find, but it's worth the price and effort. Learn their names, areas of expertise and special talents. Then find ways to reach them. Approach the wealthiest, most successful and well-connected people you know and ask them who they use and if they would be willing make introductions for you.

GUERRILLA INTELLIGENCE

Working with the best can be expensive, but working with "cheap" services is often far more expensive in the long run. It's a prudent investment to go first class because the best can:

- ➢ Save you substantial money. Experts know the ropes and exactly where to go. They've discovered all the short cuts and can get you where you want to go faster and more inexpensively than others. The best frequently can do more with a single phone call than others can produce in months of diligent efforts.
- ➢ Make you more money. The top experts know all of the latest industry buzz and developments. They know the top deals and dealmakers and what they need. Top people can put you into lucrative investments that you might never find on your own. They can also advise you on who to avoid and when to pass on an opportunity, which can save you time, money and aggravation.

GUERRILLA INTELLIGENCE (cont'd)

➤ Connect you with other top talent. Experts know other experts and have contacts who will raise the level of your game. They can move you up to a bigger and more profitable league where they play for higher stakes. The top experts can open doors and bring you into inner circles that might otherwise be closed to you.

➤ Increase your expertise. When you work with the best, your own proficiency improves. By being observant, you can learn their techniques and incorporate them into your operation.

➤ Speed your growth. Since experts can introduce you to the best people, talent and deals, you can cut out the middlemen, which will save you time and money, and fast-forward your growth. Wealthy people understand that time is money, so they cut right to the chase. Since they're in the business of making money, they're used to moving quickly and saving time.

➤ Increase your enjoyment and sense of fulfillment. When you work with the best, it's simply more fun, more exciting and more fulfilling. Working with the best can motivate you to perform at your best and reach new heights.

Whatever you hope to do has already been done in one form or another. Find a mentor who's already done what you want to do. It's inefficient to reinvent the wheel; it will only impede your progress and slow you down. Learn from them and from their experiences and know-how. Let their contacts and networks become your contacts and networks; it will speed your growth.

"ON" AND "IN" BUSINESS

As you build and lead your wealth team, think of your team members in two distinct categories. Those who work:

1.   In the business
2.   On the business

This is a concept that is a signature point of *The E-Myth Revisited: Why Most Small Businesses Don't Work and What to Do About It*, by Michael Gerber. His premise is that most people work "in" their business and get mired in the day-to-day operation. They can't get back far enough to see what's really going on. In addition, of the key areas that are required to succeed, the owner generally has expertise in only one or two. If he or she is trying to do everything alone, without delegating support functions to employees, it becomes an impossible job.

He encourages people to pull back a bit from the daily routine to look at the bigger picture and work "on" their businesses. From this perspective, they can see where they need both support and expert assistance.

Leadership of Your Wealth Team

Gerber is a great proponent of systematizing successful processes so they can be duplicated over and over. These make the business work harder, he says, so the owner doesn't have to. When someone is willing to work "on" the business, he or she can literally turn it into a cash machine. And that's what your wealth team can do for you.

For the purposes of this exercise, the term "business" is intended to mean your wealth building efforts.

Although the people on your team fall into two categories, you must lead (inspire and engage) them ALL!

The chart below provides examples of the type of assistance needed both in and on a business. You will find: (1) the type of help you have in and on your business and (2) the type of help you need in and on your business.

In My Business	**On My Business**
Bookkeepers	Corporate Attorney
Graphic Artist	Tax Strategist
Personal Assistant	Coach
Writer	Mentor
Sales Team	

Leadership of Your Wealth Team

Now that you have identified who you need on your team, let's examine the qualities you'd like members to possess. The following are some traits to consider. In the spaces below the list, feel free to add other qualities, especially if they address a special need of your business.

Here are the characteristics we look for in our team:

➤ Competent
➤ Loyal
➤ Visionary
➤ Well-focused
➤ Creative
➤ Deal-closers
➤ Hard workers
➤ Demanding (high standards and values)
➤ Honest
➤ Strong communicators
➤ Self-motivators

Your Criteria for Your Team:

_____

_____

_____

_____

_____

Before you interview and select your wealth team members, clearly identify the specific activities each member will be required to perform in and on the business. Most of your wealth team will be consulting with you on your business, but it's possible you have key individuals doing tactical work in your company as well. Check the examples below and determine what specific characteristics you hope to find in each candidate for your wealth team.

CHARACTERISTICS FOR WEALTH TEAM MEMBERS IN YOUR BUSINESS

These people provide the support services you need, the logistics to make things happen. If you're currently handling all the logistics of your own life and business, you may be holding yourself back! Think about it. If you spend the time to do work that others could do - and free you up - could you use that time to make more money? We're not talking about leisure time. We're talking about taking a serious look at what you spend your time doing every day, week or month that literally robs you of hours you could leverage in your wealth-building efforts.

Once there was a businessman on the East Coast who lived in a lovely home with beautiful grounds. He had someone to do the lawn. Someone else did the trees and an "expert" did the bushes. It might seem extravagant, but he wasn't arrogant. He didn't think it was beneath him to do yard work. Here's his simple answer: "In the time I would be mowing and trimming, I can earn far more than I pay for the help. It's much smarter for me to use my time in ways to make money than to save a little money doing things other people do better anyway."

Leadership of Your Wealth Team

Here are the characteristics we look for in our support team:

> Time-efficient
> Vision-oriented
> Service-oriented
> Responsible
> Driven by a personal vision
> Proficient at completing tasks
> Self-starters
> Team players
> Dedicated
> Share your vision

Assistant
> Is he a team player?
> What is her experience?
> Is he passionate about your business?

Bookkeeper
> Is she detail-oriented?
> How does he work with your clients?
> You have limited needs now, but when your needs grow will she be capable of filling them?
> What reports can he generate that will help you with business planning?

Office Manager
> Is she self-motivated?
> Is he detail-oriented?

Leadership of Your Wealth Team

Computer Support
- ➢ How available is she?
- ➢ Can he maintain your Web site?
- ➢ What are the in business activities she must perform?

Sales and Marketing
- ➢ Is he self-motivated?
- ➢ How would she describe her creativity?
- ➢ How well does he communicate?
- ➢ Can she achieve your revenue targets?

What other in the business characteristics do you consider important?

_____

_____

_____

_____

_____

_____

CHARACTERISTICS FOR WEALTH TEAM MEMBERS WORKING ON YOUR BUSINESS

Your wealth team is a group of your peers. They're professionals in their own right. Regardless of each one's skill and reputation, every individual must be a match for you. Here are the kinds of things we like to know about someone before we invite them to be on our wealth team. These are the people with knowledge and experience you want to leverage in your own wealth-building effort. Choose wisely.

- ➤ Is he congruent with your vision?
- ➤ Is she knowledgeable and open-minded?
- ➤ Is he detail-oriented?
- ➤ Is she willing to refer her other clients to you?
- ➤ Is he integrity driven?
- ➤ Is she willing to share her contacts with you?
- ➤ Will he buy into your vision of the business?

Financial Planner/Accountant

- ➤ What are her moral views?
- ➤ Will he advise you on his vision?
- ➤ Does she currently work on your team and give you the best advice?
- ➤ Can he work in a team context?
- ➤ Does she handle corporate returns?
- ➤ What is his area of expertise?

PR Firm

- ➤ Do they specialize in entrepreneurial venues?
- ➤ Are they well-connected?
- ➤ Are they honest?
- ➤ Are they creative?
- ➤ Are they able to understand and handle your needs?
- ➤ Are they persistent?
- ➤ Do they understand branding and good will?
- ➤ Will they be willing to work as part of a team?
- ➤ Do they understand your vision?

Leadership of Your Wealth Team

Attorney

- ➢ Is she an expert and experienced?
- ➢ Is he well-connected?
- ➢ Is she honest?
- ➢ Is he creative?
- ➢ Does she handle Nevada C corporation structures?
- ➢ Does he handle all types of corporate structures?
- ➢ Does she have experience in preparing and analyzing contacts?
- ➢ What is his vision?

Board of Directors

- ➢ Is he passionate?
- ➢ Is she well-connected?
- ➢ Is he creative?
- ➢ Does she understand your vision?
- ➢ Does he understand your needs?

Personal Coach

- ➢ Is he or she interested in helping you build your business?

What other on the business characteristics for your wealth team members do you feel are important?

_____

_____

_____

_____

_____

GUERRILLA INTERVIEW QUESTIONS

Below is a list of questions you can ask when interviewing potential members of your wealth team. This list was developed in focus groups with our top clients. Some of these questions are specific to particular members of your wealth team, such as CPAs, attorneys, financial planners and so on.

After you read the questions, create your own personalized list of interview questions. Choose those that are right for you, add your own inquiries, and then place them in the order that will bring out the information you seek.

> ➢ What is the approximate net worth of your five most affluent clients?
> ➢ In which tax bracket are most of your clients?
> ➢ Do you creatively plan new tax strategies?
> ➢ Are you familiar with any new tax and finance laws?
> ➢ Are you a team player?
> ➢ Do you have a prosperity consciousness?
> ➢ Are you a good listener?
> ➢ Do you clearly understand my vision?
> ➢ Are you self-directed?
> ➢ What five books have you read lately?
> ➢ What is your primary area of expertise?
> ➢ Do you consider intuition a sixth sense?
> ➢ Do you see yourself as highly structured?
> ➢ Once we've agreed on a direction, are you committed to achieving results in that direction?
> ➢ Is your preference to lead or follow?

Leadership of Your Wealth Team

- ➢ Are you comfortable with decision-making by consensus?
- ➢ What three accomplishments are you most proud of and why?
- ➢ How do you feel you would fit with my company and why?
- ➢ What are your beliefs as far as interacting with a team?
- ➢ What do you consider to be your best assets?
- ➢ Do you have the ability to inspire others?
- ➢ What is your net worth?
- ➢ What is your financial vision?

Create Your Own Personalized Interview Questions

Interview #1   Position: _____

_____

_____

_____

_____

_____

Interview #2   Position: _____

_____

_____

_____

_____

_____

Interview #3   Position: _____

_____

_____

_____

_____

_____

So now you've identified who needs to be on your team and how you can interview them effectively. Let's go on to leadership. How will you lead them to create the results that you're striving for?

FUTURE PACING

An essential quality of Guerrilla Leadership is the ability to see the future and design your business in a manner that will take full advantage of the benefits you envisioned. Guerrilla Leadership is proactive: you must initiate action as opposed to just reacting to whatever occurs. You must be in front, in the lead, at the helm - not catching up. Guerrilla Leaders anticipate surprises instead of feeling that they were dropped on them. We call this process, "future pacing."

Future pacing is the ability to look down the road - six months, 12 months, three years, five years or longer - and lead your team now to achieve your objectives:

Leadership of Your Wealth Team

➤On time
➤On target
➤Solidly in the black (profitable)

Look at your marketing plan. What should you do to future pace your business? Remember, as the leader, it's up to you to pace the work . . . not do the work! You make sure everyone else does their job, on time, on target and profitably.

GUERRILLA TACTIC

A good format for future pacing is:

1. Quantify your target revenue. Identify how much money you hope to make (remember Napoleon Hill's advice - you must be exceptionally clear). Express the amount in precise dollar amounts. For example, $97,500 net profit in six months.

2. Identify the strategies now in place that will produce your target revenue.

3. Identify the tactics that will support your strategy.

4. Identify the people that you'll lead who will do the work.

Even though these points cover some ground that we've previously addressed, fully complete all four steps - but focus on future pacing. You may be surprised by the concentrated effort and time it'll take you to fully complete these steps. Just know it will pay off in the long run.

Leadership of Your Wealth Team

Future pacing also requires you to examine and anticipate the details. Future pacing your assets means looking at real estate deals, stock purchases and other investments. Future pacing is essential for leaders to make their businesses consistently profitable. Learn to examine the future, anticipate coming events, and structure your business and wealth building accordingly.

LEADERSHIP VS. MANAGEMENT

You lead a wealth team; you don't manage it. These peers should be selected because they are self-managers. Don't insult them by micromanaging them. Since those on your wealth team will be professionals, getting them onboard with your vision and aligned with your goals will be easy. When you're paying for their services, they'll be eager to serve you in the best way possible.

Today, these professionals are trained to work with you in a cooperative way. It was only in the Industrial Age that "experts" were often bullies and got away with it! Today, cooperation is the hallmark of professional relationships. If someone is overbearing or puts down your vision, do what we do: trade up. You don't need that.

Here are the characteristics we demand of ourselves and our wealth team.

Leadership of Your Wealth Team

The "5 C's of Leadership" are:

1. Character
2. Capacity
3. Credibility
4. Courage
5. Communication

If a person doesn't have these core traits, it doesn't matter what their skill level is in their field. We simply won't work with them. Let's further examine what the "5 C's" of leadership are.

Character

A leader must have strong character, those qualities that followers will respond to. Character is your internal makeup; your personal DNA. Are you strong, decisive, mellow, thoughtful, assertive, good-natured or driven?

Capacity

A leader must have the ability to accomplish what he or she conceives or believes. Capacity enables leaders to internalize their visions and express them in ways that make others give their enthusiastic support.

Credibility

Credibility means that the leader is believable. Team members won't sacrifice themselves for leaders whom they don't believe. Personal integrity underlies credibility. Credibility is established through actions as opposed to words.

Leadership of Your Wealth Team

Courage

Courage is the inner strength required to overcome obstacles, stay on track and move your vision forward.

> *"Courage is fear that has said its prayers."*
> Karl Barth
> Swiss Theologian

Communication

Communication is the manner in which you put your vision into action. It's explaining your vision to others and enlisting their help and support.

Communication is the single most important skill in dealing with your wealth team. If you're vague in your requests for information, don't return phone calls or are slow to follow up, you reduce the team's ability to help you reach your financial goals. Poor communication on your part lowers the level of performance of the whole team. It's a bad model.

Rank yourself on each of the five qualities of leadership. Use a scale of 1-10 with 1 being the lowest. In the spaces provided below, write what you must do to improve in each area.

Character

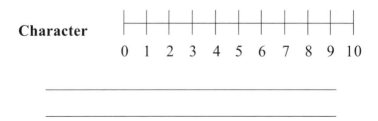

0 1 2 3 4 5 6 7 8 9 10

_____

_____

Leadership of Your Wealth Team

Capacity

0 1 2 3 4 5 6 7 8 9 10

_____

_____

Credibility

0 1 2 3 4 5 6 7 8 9 10

_____

_____

Courage

0 1 2 3 4 5 6 7 8 9 10

_____

_____

Communication

0 1 2 3 4 5 6 7 8 9 10

_____

_____

COMMUNICATION FOR LEADERS

Since communication with your wealth team is key, here are three effective ways to improve your communication skills:

1. The power of questions.
2. Action through accountability.
3. Inquiries to solutions.

1. Power of questions

Questions stimulate the strategic side of the brain and cause people to think. They also keep us engaged. When we're asked open-ended questions, such as "what" and "how," our brains are roused into action and driven to come up with answers. For example:

> ➢ What will you do?
> ➢ What do you want?
> ➢ What will the impact be?
> ➢ How will you do it?
> ➢ How does it impact our strategy?
> ➢ How will it impact our revenue?

When you ask questions of your team members, it signifies that you value their responses, which gives them a stake in the outcome. Questioning also frequently results in better solutions, especially when those questioned have special knowledge and the ability to provide outstanding suggestions.

Leadership of Your Wealth Team

2. Accountability through action

Progress is made faster when everyone is on the same page and knows what's expected. Your wealth team will be more efficient if the measurable results of any action are clear. It can be very simple to set up tracking for any project or task you request from a wealth team member. Remember, the more efficient you are, the better use you'll make of everyone's time. That saves you money! Use the same formula to keep yourself on track.

1	2	3	4
What	**What**	**With Whom**	**With Whom**
What is the task to be completed?	When does it need to be finished?	With whom do you need to connect?	Who will hold you accountable?

GUERRILLA TACTIC

To help support your goals, establish accountability partners to keep your team focused and on track. Accountability partners lend their support to assure that the mission is accomplished as scheduled. For example, an accountability partner would state, "George, I know you're committed to this project and the deadline is quickly approaching.

GUERRILLA TACTIC (cont'd)

> ➢ Tell me, step-by-step, precisely what you still need to complete.
> ➢ Do you need to renegotiate with the team?
> ➢ How can I support you?
> ➢ Do you need additional help?

Create supportive partners, not blame partners, as so many managers do. Don't create fall guys. In accountability partnerships, the questioner's main goal is to prompt and support the partner's intention. It's a type of internal review that keeps team members focused and on track. When others take an active partnership interest in outcomes, it gives the partners who must perform the bulk of the work others with whom they can consult, approach for advice or simply speak.

3. Inquiry to solution

As the leader, you must be responsive to the team members to keep the action moving forward. Ask:

A. What do you need?
B. When do you need it?
C. Is there something you would like me to do?

When team members stray off course, as they will, the goal of an effective leader is to bring them back on course and reenergize them. This usually means finding solutions, rather than dwelling on problems.

Leadership of Your Wealth Team

SUCCESS STORIES

Dawn Weightman

"Instead of surrounding myself with people who doubt my abilities and their own, I've created a team of qualified professionals who have the tactical expertise that will help me. I've learned to look at their actions and results, not their words.

Prior to my divorce, I was making good money as a hotel executive, but my husband handled all my personal finances. Suddenly, after the divorce, I was outside, looking in, and wondering where all my wealth went. So, I decided to get smart and start playing the financial game.

At first, I was a Lone Ranger, who lacked confidence. Rather than risk appearing to be ignorant, I held back. Then, I decided to build a good team to support me. Instead of consulting friends who had no special expertise, I interviewed and hired professionals - attorneys, tax accountants, investors, brokers, and experts who had experience in areas that I lacked. I sought out the best people on the basis of the results they had produced and by examining their professional accomplishments.

With their help, I gave $200,000 of my hemorrhaging IRA to a real estate developer in Dallas. In a year, its value has jumped to over $500,000. When I deal with my team, I'm in charge and I'm very specific about what I want. I make sure to ask all the right qualifying questions to get the good opportunities. Now that I've built a team I totally enjoy working with, I've almost doubled my portfolio in less than 18 months."

Leadership of Your Wealth Team

SUMMING UP

Millionaires assemble great teams, so follow their example and surround yourself with the best people. However, remember - you must be the team leader. As the leader, learn how to future pace, which means developing the ability to see the future - 6 months, 12 months, three years, five years or longer - and design your business in a manner that'll take full advantage of the benefits you want.

Leadership must be proactive. Initiate action; don't just react to the actions of others or circumstances. Learn how to clearly communicate by asking questions. Create accountability through action by making sure that each team member understands:

➤ The precise task to be completed,
➤ When it must be finished,
➤ With whom he or she needs to connect, and
➤ Who will hold him or her accountable.

Leadership of Your Wealth Team

LORAL'S LEARNING LOOP

What are three things you learned from this chapter?

_____

_____

_____

_____

_____

_____

What three actions will you take as a result of this chapter?

_____

_____

_____

_____

_____

_____

List the dates when you will begin and complete your three actions.

_____

_____

_____

Leadership of Your Wealth Team

To whom will you be accountable?

_____

_____

Section IV

PUTTING
IT ALL
TOGETHER

9

Integration and Action

We've reached the end . . . and it's time to start at the beginning!

By that we mean, even though this book was written as a workbook, you – like most people – may have read the entire book first without completing any of the written forms. Candidly, most books don't call for action. This one almost demands it.

We wrote this book because we know there are individuals – and we hope you're among them – who are willing to stop in their tracks, turn in a new direction and start building wealth.

So the first thing we want to do is congratulate you for getting through the book. As we know all too well at Live Out Loud, it's very difficult to break old training and start talking about money. Also, money is a highly charged subject and it takes some personal strength to plow through—while your old ideas, fears and failures threaten to overload your system.

If we've done our job, you have no doubt that there's a distinct difference between the old Industrial Age model and the new Information Age model. You can see that you don't have to flounder alone. Better yet, we trust we've shown that you – yes, you – can reach sustainable wealth that will support you for a lifetime and provide a legacy for your family if you choose. You can reach financial freedom even if you're currently in debt. Many of our clients have!

Integration and Action

You see, if you don't really get the vision – that inner knowing – that wealth is possible, the book is just ink on paper. But if the concepts we introduced you to got you excited, made your imagination flicker a bit brighter and allowed you to see the possibilities for yourself, then commit to follow through.

This short chapter is called "Integration and Action." We're going to tell you right now that you need to take action first. One step . . . another . . . and another. Then you'll begin to internalize and integrate the guerrilla tactics we've introduced.

The first action we invite you to take is to turn to Chapter 10. We highlight the options available through Live Out Loud and related programs.

The next action will begin the process of integration of the information into your mind, heart and life. Review the book and, this time, actually do the exercises, write your notes and put pen to paper to make this information your own.

So welcome to the end of the book, and the beginning of your guerrilla wealth future!

Jay Conrad Levinson
Loral Langemeier

SUCCESS STORIES

Richard and Theresa Banta

"Prior to meeting Loral Langemeier, we never thought much about money since we always had cash available. I'm a criminal defense lawyer and Theresa has a successful graphic design business. In the context of wealth building, we had done little planning.

After we each attended Loral's Big Table, where we were introduced to her wealth building strategies, we converted our home of 18 years into a rental property and bought a completely remodeled, old Victorian. We then moved our offices to the Victorian, which immediately saved us $1,200 that we had been paying for office space.

Now, we're in the process of buying a house with people from the Big Table in New York. We bought a house through Loral's Get Real, Inc. and we're in the process of buying a house in Denver that is appraised for substantially more than we're paying. The important thing is that we're taking action: you can know all the steps to take, but it is all about taking action.

We also created a strong wealth team. Our bankers are in place and we have new mortgage lenders, a new CPA and a new bookkeeper. Theresa has also hired a new design assistant so she can work on her business instead of in it, which frees her to concentrate more on real estate.

Our business model is diversified with real estate, stocks and a network marketing business. We're also

Integration and Action

launching a new business and Web site called 'Wealth Ready Go' to teach others what we learned from Loral. We now have four different legal entities, one for each business we're operating.

We started with $200,000 equity in our old house, which we still have, plus we've gained about $60,000 equity in our new home. Our passive income went from zero to about 25 percent of our revenue. In a year, we've easily doubled our net worth and we're absolutely confident that it will redouble and go from 25 percent to 50 percent in passive income. It's about being able to make money while we sleep."

10

What's Next?

The next thing we want to do is extend once again our offer to help you get started on your way to wealth with a free Action Strategy Session. These 20-minute sessions – a $150 value – will give you one-on-one time with a Strategist trained by Loral. Each Strategist is skilled in quickly determining where you are and what your next steps should be, depending on your financial situation, your goals and your current level of financial expertise.

ACTION ITEM 1

Call to schedule your FREE Action Strategy Session – 1-888-262-2402.

ACTION ITEM 2

Visit www.liveoutloud.com

Live Out Loud is a core program to get you in the conversation about money. You'll see that the Live Out Loud program is an extension of *Guerrilla Wealth*. It's the place where people begin to get in the game.

Live Out Loud Personal Wealth Coaching

Get the one-on-one help you want. For more details visit www.liveoutloudcoaching.com.

Wealth Diva: A Man Is Not a Plan! For Women Only!

The Wealth Diva program is designed to provide the same kind of financial literacy and wealth training in a format designed for women only. Visit www.wealthdiva.com.

Loral's Big Table—For Business Owners/Investors

This is for true entrepreneurial wealth builders. Loral's Big Table is the place to learn and apply the nuts and bolts of wealth building to enhance your investing strategy. This is where players meet and discuss real estate, business and much more. Enrollment in each Big Table is limited. This invitation-only program isn't for everyone. To find out more or to apply, visit www.loralsbigtable.com.

Get Real Wealth Training and Coaching

Those interested in building a substantial real estate portfolio while learning advanced techniques can enroll in one-on-one coaching at www.getrealcoaching.com. Loral also takes investors to the streets of Philadelphia where she and her partner conduct the Get Real Tour. Details are available at www.getrealinc.net.

If you're looking for a charity, we at Live Out Loud have a top choice ... www.life-school.org

Ready. Go!